JN236890

New Version対応

新TOEIC® TEST
英文法・語彙
スピード マスター

安河内 哲也 著

Jリサーチ出版

TOEIC is a registered trademark of Educational Testing Service（ETS）.
This publication is not endorsed or approved by ETS.

はじめに

　本書は、TOEIC TESTのPart 5やPart 6で頻出の問題形式に的を絞り、効率よくポイントがマスターできるように作成された学習書です。
　近年のTOEICでは、いくつかの文法分野、および語法・語彙の問題に出題が集中しています。本書では、それらの出題分野を絞り込んで分類——品詞、代名詞、時制・準動詞、形容詞・副詞、動詞、名詞、接続詞・前置詞という7つの分野に分類——したものと、最後にPart6対策とを合わせて292問の練習問題、さらに巻末には52問の模擬試験問題（計344問）を通じて、**TOEICでよく問われるパターンを徹底練習**します。
　TOEICで試される文法ポイント自体は、大学受験や英検1級などのさまざまな検定試験と比較しても、決して難しいものではありません。TOEICの難しさの原因は、じつは問題文にあるのです。そこで、本書では高得点を狙う皆さんの練習となるよう、TOEIC TESTレベルと同等か、それ以上のレベルのビジネス文例を用いて問題を作成しています。
　また、TOEICをすでに経験したことのある皆さんはお分かりのとおり、問題のポイントを正確につかみ取るためには、英文全体の大枠——主語や述語動詞などといったもろもろ——を、素早く的確に読み取る必要があります。
　特に、語彙問題の出題対象は無限にあるわけですから、**頻度の高い語彙の暗記に加えて、全体の構造から「考えて解く」習慣をつけることが高得点をとるための鉄則**になります。従って本書では、文の主構造を図解し、節の役割を記号で示すことにより、文法的思考力と読解力の錬成を目指します。
　もちろん本書で学習する内容は、Part 5やPart 6以外の問題を解くための地力養成としても有効です。頻出問題を追いかけ、答えを確認するだけの学習ではなく、本書が、根本的な実力養成のための英語学習の一助となれば幸いです。
　問題作成においては、複数のネイティブスピーカーの皆さんの助力をいただきました。特にCraig Brantley氏には多大なるご尽力をいただきました。これらの皆様に感謝いたします。
　皆様のTOEIC TEST、および英語学習での成功を願います。

安河内哲也

Contents

はじめに ……………………………………………………………… 3
本書の利用法 ………………………………………………………… 5
構造分析に使用する記号 …………………………………………… 6

英文法・語彙スピードマスター　トレーニング編 ……………… 9

Lesson 1　文型に即した品詞の選択 ……………………………… 10
　　　　　　Exercises ……………………………………………… 12

Lesson 2　文型に適した代名詞・関係詞の選択 ………………… 32
　　　　　　Exercises ……………………………………………… 36

Lesson 3　適した動詞形の選択 …………………………………… 56
　　　　　　Exercises ……………………………………………… 60

Lesson 4　意味や用法が適した形容詞・副詞の選択 …………… 80
　　　　　　Exercises ……………………………………………… 82

Lesson 5　意味や用法が適した名詞の選択 ……………………… 102
　　　　　　Exercises ……………………………………………… 104

Lesson 6　意味や用法が適した動詞の選択 ……………………… 124
　　　　　　Exercises ……………………………………………… 126

Lesson 7　意味や用法が適した接続詞・前置詞・論理マーカーの選択 …… 146
　　　　　　Exercises ……………………………………………… 148

Lesson 8　Part6対策 ……………………………………………… 168
　　　　　　Exercises ……………………………………………… 170

TOEIC® TEST　英文法・語彙模擬試験 ……………………… 187
正解と解説 …………………………………………………………… 202

◆最重要接尾辞一覧 ………………………………………………… 186

本書の利用法

　本書はTOEICの直前対策を念頭に、文法・語彙問題の練習を徹底的に行うための1冊です。たくさんの問題を**1問20秒**で解きながら、頻出パターンを熟知していただくことが本書の目的です。

☞英文法・語彙スピードマスター　トレーニング編

　本書では近年の出題形式を分析し、文法・語彙のジャンルを7つの項目に分けました（Lesson1 ～ 7）。そして最後のLesson8ではPart6の問題演習を行います。いずれのLessonでもまず最初に学習のポイント＝文法・語彙事項の頻出パターンを紹介します。これを頭に入れてからEXERCISESに挑戦してください。

　EXERCISESは、TOEICのPart5（短文空所補充問題）とPart6（長文空所補充問題）と同じスタイルの練習問題で構成。**Lesson1 ～ 7は各40問**で、問題と正解を照合しやすいように、左ページに問題、右ページに正解・解説という見開き展開を採用しています。**Lesson8**ではPart6と同じ形式の問題を**4つ（計12問）**用意しました。スピードを意識しながらEXERCISESを全て解き、正解を確認しましょう。

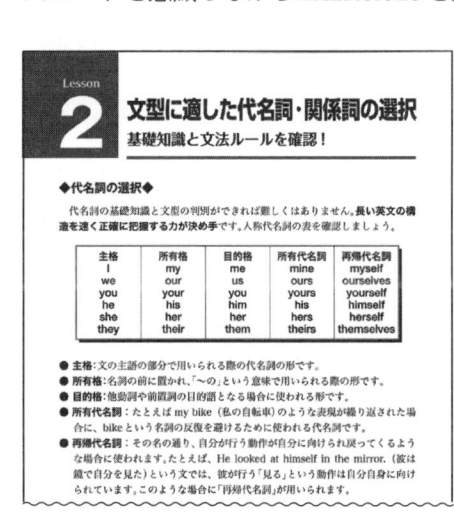

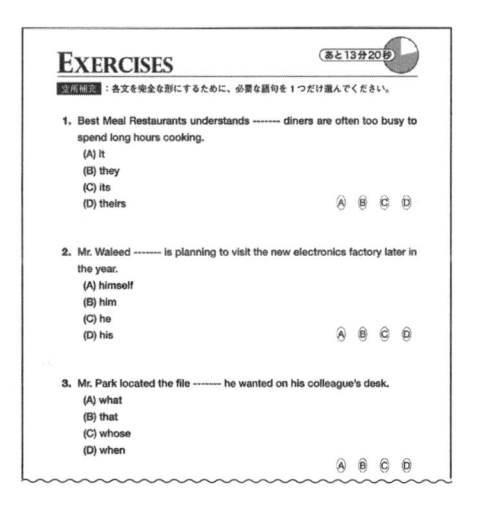

☞TOEIC® TEST英文法・語彙模擬試験

　総仕上げのために、実際のTOEICに合わせて、短文空所補充問題（Part5）40問と長文空所補充問題（Part6）12問で構成。**1問20秒、17分20秒**での完答目指して頑張りましょう。

構造分析に使用する記号

本書 EXERCISES の「正解・解説」内の「構造」部分で使用されている記号の意味を以下に記します。

名詞の働きをするもの
⇒該当する名詞の働きをする部分を [ ] で囲む。

◆動名詞
I like [**surfing the Internet**].
私は [インターネットを見て回ること] が好きだ。
We look forward to [**having an early reply from you**].
私たちは [あなたから早いご返事があること] を楽しみにしています。

◆不定詞の名詞的用法
Our first priority is [**to maintain the quality of the product**].
我々の最優先事項は、[製品の品質を維持すること] だ。
It is hard [**to motivate the part-timers**].
[非常勤社員たちにやる気を起こさせること] は困難である。

◆疑問詞＋不定詞
I asked the teller [**how to fill in the form**].
私は窓口係に [その用紙をどうやって記入するか] を尋ねた。
Do you know [**where to save this file**]?
[このファイルをどこに保存すればいいか] 知っていますか。

◆that節「SがVするということ」
I think [**that the third plan is the best**].
私は [第3案が一番よい] と思う。
It is true [**that the company is in danger of bankruptcy**].
[その会社が倒産の危機にあるということ] は本当だ。

◆if節「SがVするかどうか」
I don't know [**if the meeting has already finished**].
私は [会議がもう終わったかどうか] 知りません。
Can you tell me [**if you have this item in stock**]?
[この品の在庫があるかどうか] 私に教えてもらえますか。

◆疑問詞節
Do you know [**who is going to chair the conference**]?
あなたは [誰が会議の司会をする予定か] 知っていますか。
I don't remember [**where I left the master key**].
私は [マスターキーをどこに置いたか] 覚えていない。

◆関係代名詞の what 節
[**What I need most**] is an efficient secretary.
[私が最も必要としているもの] は有能な秘書だ。

[What he said] is to the point.
［彼が言ったこと］は的を射ている。

形容詞の働きをするもの
⇒修飾される名詞を □、形容詞の働きをするものを＜　＞で囲む。

◆前置詞＋名詞
The rent ＜of my apartment＞ is fairly high.
＜私のアパートの＞ 家賃 はかなり高い。
The stock price ＜of the company＞ is soaring.
＜その会社の＞ 株価 は急騰している。

◆不定詞の形容詞的用法
I need some time ＜to think about the problem＞.
私は＜その問題について考える＞ 時間 が必要だ。
This is a powerful tool ＜to get rid of spam mail＞.
これは＜迷惑メールを排除するための＞ 強力な方法 です。

◆現在分詞
The street is crowed with people ＜watching the parade＞.
通りは＜パレードを見ている＞ 人々 で混雑している。
Tom was irritated at the bell ＜ringing without a break＞.
トムは＜止むことなく鳴り続ける＞ ベル にイライラした。

◆過去分詞
This is a term ＜used in the publishing trade＞.
これは＜出版業界で使われている＞ 用語 です。
A man ＜named Maeda＞ came to see you.
＜マエダという名前の＞ 男性 があなたに会いに来ました。

◆関係代名詞節
She is a good leader ＜who is respected by all the staff members＞.
彼女は＜スタッフ全員から尊敬されている＞ 優秀なリーダー だ。
The computer ＜that I bought last month＞ has broken down.
＜私が先月買った＞ パソコン が故障した。
This book is intended for people ＜whose mother tongue is not English＞.
これは＜母国語が英語ではない＞ 人々 に向けて書かれた本です。

◆関係副詞節
I don't know the time ＜when the train leaves＞.
私は＜電車が出発する＞ 時間 を知らない。
New York is the city ＜where I want to work＞.
ニューヨークは＜私が働きたい＞ 都市 だ。

同格の働きをするもの

⇒説明される名詞を□、同格説明の部分を＜　＞で囲む。

◆同格のthat節

There is a good chance <that we will get a pay raise>.
＜我々が昇給するという＞ かなりの見込み がある。

The news <that the negotiation failed> disappointed the CEO.
＜交渉が失敗したという＞ 知らせ はCEOを落胆させた。

◆カンマによる同格補足

They set up a new office in Bern, <the capital of Switzerland>.
彼らは＜スイスの首都である＞ ベルン に新事務所を設立した。

I met John, <a former colleague of mine>.
私は＜元同僚の＞ ジョン に会った。

副詞の働きをするもの

⇒該当する副詞の働きをする部分を（　）で囲む。

◆前置詞＋名詞

She has made great progress (in speaking English).
彼女は(英会話において)大きく進歩した。
He went to Moscow (on business).
彼は(仕事で)モスクワへ行った。

◆分詞構文（Ving）

(Hearing the news), the director turned pale.
(その知らせを聞いて)重役は青ざめた。
(Having lived in the U.S.), he speaks English fluently.
(米国に住んでいたので)彼は英語を流ちょうに話す。

◆受動分詞構文（Vpp）

(Seen from the sky), the islands look really beautiful.
(空から見られたとき)その島々は本当に美しく見える。
(Compared with his predecessor), our new boss is harder on us.
(前任者と比較されたとき)新しい上司の方が我々に厳しい。

◆従属接続詞＋ＳＶ

(Although they reduced the price), the sales have been sluggish.
(彼らは値下げをしたけれども)売り上げはずっと芳しくない。
The product is selling well (because it was introduced on TV).
(テレビで紹介されたので)その製品はよく売れている。

◆不定詞の副詞的用法

I am glad (to make your acquaintance).
(あなたとお知り合いになれて)私は嬉しいです。
(To start a business), you need a considerable sum of money.
(商売を始めるためには)君はかなりの大金が必要だ。

英文法・語彙
スピードマスター

トレーニング編

　まずはLesson1～7で、文法・語彙の頻出7分野について学習しましょう。各Lessonでは、最初に学習のポイントや注意点を頭に入れてから、EXERCISESにチャレンジしてみてください。EXERCISESはそれぞれ40問、1問を20秒平均で解くように時間を意識してやってみましょう。Lesson8ではPart6の対策について学びます。EXERCISESは小問3つを含む文章を4つ用意しました。それぞれを1分のペースで解き進みましょう。

Lesson 1 文型に即した品詞の選択
文全体の構造を正確に把握！

　文型に即した品詞を選択するタイプの問題では、まず文全体の構造を正確に把握する必要があります。その**全体の構造から、空所に入る単語がどのような品詞になるのかを判別します**。おなじみの基本5文型に照らして品詞を分類すると、以下のようになります。

> S（主語）………名詞
> V（述語動詞）…動詞
> O（目的語）……名詞
> C（補語）………名詞および形容詞
> M（修飾語）……副詞（および名詞を直接修飾する形容詞）

◆動詞か形容詞かを選択する◆

> 例題：The general manager, upon entering the office, ------- that it was
> 　　　　　S　　　　　　　　　　　　　　　　　　　　　　　　　V　　　　　O
> 　　　comfortable for everybody to work in.
>
> 　　　(A) commented　　(B) commentary　　(C) commenting　　(D) comment

正解　**(A)**

訳　部長は、オフィスに入るとすぐに、そこは誰もが働くのに適していると言った。

【解説】この文の中で、空所の部分は文全体の述語動詞の働きをしています。そこで「名詞」や「形容詞」ではなく、当然動詞の選択となり、名詞の(B) commentaryを消去することができるわけです。(C) commentingのようなing形も単独では動詞となることができないため、答えにはなりません。また、(D) commentだと三単現のs（または過去形のed）が必要なため、やはり答えにはなりません。

　このように、品詞を選択するタイプの問題では**空所の部分が文の中でどのような要素になっているのかに気をつけて答えを絞っていくことが重要**です。

◆形容詞か副詞かを選択する◆

> 例題：The regional manager asked the supervisor from headquarters to assess the employees according to their ------- positions.
> S   V   O   V'   O'   M
>
> (A) individuality (B) individually (C) individual (D) individuals

正解　(C)

訳　地域部長は本部からの監督者に対し、それぞれの地位に従って従業員を評価するよう依頼した。

【解説】文の要素としてはMですが、その中の一部を問うている問題ですから、空所の前後の部分から判断します。空所の直後にはpositionsという名詞があり、空所の部分はこの名詞を修飾しています。名詞を修飾するのは形容詞ですから、名詞以外の品詞を修飾するために使われる副詞は答えにはならないわけです。したがって(B)individuallyはまず消去することができます。(A)individualityや(D)individualsは名詞なので、文意に合いません。形容詞の(C)individualが正解となります。この単語は形容詞としても名詞としても使われますが、(D)には複数形のsがついているため、名詞として使われているとわかります。

このような品詞の判別の手がかりになるのが、選択肢の単語の語尾（接尾辞）です。形容詞と副詞に関しては以下のルールをしっかりと覚えておいてください。

| 形容詞 + ly = 副詞 | respective（形容詞） + ly | =respectively（副詞） |
| 名詞 + ly = 形容詞 | friend（名詞） + ly | =friendly（形容詞） |

また、名詞を作る接尾辞と形容詞を作る接尾辞の大まかな傾向を知っておくことも役に立ちます。

| 形容詞を作る主な接尾辞 | -ful, -able, -cial, -ant, -ive, -ic, -ious, -eous |
| 名詞を作る主な接尾辞 | -ment, -tion, -sion, -ce, -ity, -ness |

品詞の判別に関して、上記で示した様々な方法は役に立つものの、やはり、**個別の単語およびその派生語を、品詞や用法に注意しながら学び増やしていくことが、このタイプの問題での得点力を高めるためには最も重要**です。個別の問題を解きながら語彙を増やしていきましょう。

EXERCISES

空所補充：各文を完全な形にするために、必要な語句を1つだけ選んでください。

1. Although offering only modest -------, the Haven Hotel is popular with executives because of its proximity to Auckland's main airport.
   (A) accommodate
   (B) accommodations
   (C) accommodating
   (D) accommodated

2. Gulf Industries is considered an especially ------- Saudi company that regularly innovates in the field of petroleum products.
   (A) rely
   (B) reliance
   (C) reliable
   (D) relying

3. Yeoh Accounting's analyst trainee program is widely regarded as one of the most ------- challenging in Singapore.
   (A) intellect
   (B) intellectually
   (C) intellectual
   (D) intellectualism

4. Cibi Resorts Athens reported room rentals were up as more families from China and India became interested in taking ------- European vacations.
   (A) exclude
   (B) excluding
   (C) exclusive
   (D) exclusion

全部で40問あります。1問20秒、13分20秒での完答を目指して挑戦しましょう。
すべて解答してから＜正解と解説＞と照合してください。

1. 正解 (B)

【解説】offer（提供する）という他動詞の目的語となり、modest（質素な）という形容詞で修飾されている部分なので、名詞のaccommodations（宿泊設備）が適当。-tionは名詞を作る接尾辞。

構造 (Although offering only modest accommodations), the Haven Hotel ₍s₎ is ₍v₎ popular ₍c₎ (with executives) (because of its proximity ⟨to Auckland's main airport⟩).

【訳】質素な宿泊施設しか提供していないものの、Haven Hotelは、Aucklandの主要な空港に近いために、重役に人気がある。

- accommodate 動 適応させる
- accommodated accommodateの過去（分詞）形
- executive 名 重役
- accommodating accommodateの現在分詞形
- be popular with ～ 熟 ～に人気がある
- proximity to ～ 熟 ～に近いこと

2. 正解 (C)

【解説】Saudi companyという名詞を修飾する部分が空所なので、形容詞のreliable（信頼できる）が正解。-ableという接尾辞は「…できる」という意味の形容詞を作る。

構造 Gulf Industries ₍s₎ is considered ₍v₎ an especially reliable Saudi company ₍c₎ ⟨that regularly innovates (in the field ⟨of petroleum products⟩)⟩.

【訳】Gulf Industriesは石油製品の分野で絶えず技術革新をしている、特に信頼のおけるサウジアラビアの企業であると考えられている。

- rely 動 信頼する
- regularly 副 定期的に
- reliance 名 依存
- innovate 動 革新する
- relying relyの現在分詞形
- petroleum 名 石油

3. 正解 (B)

【解説】形容詞challenging（やりがいのある）を修飾する部分なので、副詞を選択する。intellectual（知的な）という形容詞に接尾辞の-lyが付いた副詞のintellectually（知的に）が正解。

構造 Yeoh Accounting's analyst trainee program ₍s₎ is widely regarded ₍v₎ (as one ⟨of the most intellectually challenging ⟨in Singapore⟩⟩).

【訳】Yeoh会計のアナリスト養成プログラムは、シンガポールで最も知的要求の高いものの一つであると広く認知されている。

- intellect 名 知性
- analyst 名 分析者
- intellectualism 名 知性偏重
- trainee 名 研修生
- accounting 名 会計

4. 正解 (C)

【解説】European vacationという名詞句を修飾する部分なので、形容詞exclusive（高級な）を選ぶ。-iveは主に形容詞を作る接尾辞。

構造 Cibi Resorts Athens ₍s₎ reported ₍v₎ [room rentals were up (as more families ⟨from China and India⟩ became interested (in [taking exclusive European vacations]))].

【訳】Cibiリゾート・アテネは、高級なヨーロッパでの旅行に興味を持つ中国やインドからの家族旅行者が増えるにつれ、部屋の稼働率は上がっていると報告した。

- exclude 動 除外する
- excluding excludeの現在分詞形
- exclusion 名 除外

文型に即した品詞の選択

5. Reservations at Al el-Sheikh Hotel are up 12% due to ------- wet weather at rival vacation destinations.
   (A) dismay
   (B) dismays
   (C) dismayed
   (D) dismayingly

6. At the ticket counter, passengers are asked to present their official ------- authorizing international travel.
   (A) documentary
   (B) documentation
   (C) documentarily
   (D) documenting

7. After overseeing the electronics division, Mr. Gu was offered a quick ------- over his colleagues to the post of regional manager.
   (A) promotionally
   (B) promotional
   (C) promoted
   (D) promotion

8. The introduction of fuel-efficient transmissions has ------- changed the way the automobile industry operates over the past 30 years.
   (A) comprehensively
   (B) comprehend
   (C) comprehending
   (D) comprehensive

5. 正解　(D)

【解説】dismay はもともと「がっかりさせる」という意味の動詞。これが dismaying という現在分詞形になると、「がっかりさせる；残念な」という形容詞として用いられる。これに、接尾辞の -ly が付くと dismayingly（残念なほどに）という副詞になる。空所は形容詞の wet を修飾する部分なので副詞の dismayingly が適当。dismayed は dismay の過去（分詞）形。

構造 Reservations ₛ ⟨at Al el-Sheikh Hotel⟩ are ᵥ up 12% ᴄ (due to dismayingly wet weather ⟨at rival vacation destinations⟩).

【訳】Al el-Sheikh ホテルの予約率は、競争相手のリゾート地の陰鬱なほど雨がちな天気のために、12%上昇している。

- □ due to ~　熟 ~のために
- □ rival　形 競合の
- □ vacation destination　名 リゾート地

6. 正解　(B)

【解説】present という他動詞の目的語となり、また形容詞 official が修飾する部分が空所なので、名詞の documentation（文書）が適当。authorizing 以降は分詞の形容詞的用法による修飾部分。-tion は名詞を作る接尾辞。

構造 (At the ticket counter), passengers ₛ are asked ᵥ to present their official documentation ⟨authorizing international travel⟩.

【訳】チケットカウンターにおいて、乗客は外国旅行を許可する正式な書類を提示することが求められる。

- □ documentary　形 文書の
- □ documentarily　副 記録資料的に
- □ documenting　document の現在分詞形
- □ passenger　名 乗客
- □ present　動 提示する
- □ authorize　動 許可する

7. 正解　(D)

【解説】quick という形容詞が修飾する部分が空所なので、名詞の promotion（昇進）が適当。-tion は名詞を作る接尾辞。

構造 (After [overseeing the electronics division]), Mr. Gu ₛ was offered ᵥ a quick promotion ⟨over his colleagues⟩ ⟨to the post ⟨of regional manager⟩⟩.

【訳】電子機器部門の監督を務めた後、Gu 氏は、同僚に先んじて地域担当マネージャーへの昇進を打診された。

- □ promotionally　副 宣伝用に
- □ promotional　形 販売促進の
- □ promoted　promote の過去（分詞）形
- □ oversee　動 監督する
- □ electronics division　名 電子機器部門
- □ offer　動 申し出る
- □ colleague　名 同僚
- □ post　名 地位
- □ regional　形 地域の

8. 正解　(A)

【解説】動詞 change を修飾する部分が空所なので、副詞の comprehensively（総合的に）が適当。これは comprehensive（総合的な）という形容詞に接尾辞の -ly が付いて副詞になったもの。

構造 The introduction ₛ ⟨of fuel-efficient transmissions⟩ has (comprehensively) changed ᵥ [ₒ the way the automobile industry operates (over the past 30 years)].

【訳】燃料効率のよい変速機の導入により、過去30年に及んで、自動車産業の活動は全般的に変化してきた。

- □ comprehend　動 理解する
- □ comprehending　comprehend の現在分詞形
- □ fuel-efficient　形 燃料効率のよい
- □ transmission　名 変速機
- □ automobile industry　名 自動車産業
- □ operate　動 経営する

9. All sales representatives will be given reasonable ------- for their business-related expenses.
   (A) allowances
   (B) allowable
   (C) allowably
   (D) allow

10. The EcoStar Sprint automobile retails for just $9,999, making it ------- among consumers looking for inexpensive yet low-emission cars.
    (A) popularly
    (B) popularity
    (C) popular
    (D) popularize

11. Professor Kalima's book, *Risks and Opportunities*, ------- addresses emerging forces in the global farming sector.
    (A) suited
    (B) suiting
    (C) suit
    (D) suitably

12. Chief Financial Officer John Xiu presented some insightful ------- of the company's cash position at the board meeting.
    (A) analyzes
    (B) analytically
    (C) analyst
    (D) analyses

9. 正解 (A)

【解説】reasonable（妥当な）という形容詞が修飾する部分が空所なのでallowances（手当）という名詞が適当。-ableは「…できる」という意味の形容詞を作る接尾辞。

構造 All sales representatives ⓢ will be given ⓥ reasonable allowances (for their business-related expenses).

【訳】すべての販売担当者は仕事関係の出費に関しては妥当な手当を受けるであろう。

- □ allowable　　　㊄許される　　　□ allowably　　㊄差し支えなく　　□ allow　　㊄許す
- □ sales representative　㊄販売員　　□ reasonable　㊄正当な；ほどよい　□ business-related　㊄ビジネスに関連した
- □ expenses　　　㊄経費

10. 正解 (C)

【解説】make O C（OをCにする）という表現のCの部分を補充する。itはthe EcoStar Sprint automobileを指しており、これを形容する形容詞のpopular（人気のある）が正解となる。

構造 The EcoStar Sprint automobile ⓢ retails ⓥ (for just $9,999), (making it popular (among consumers ⟨looking for inexpensive yet low-emission cars⟩)).

【訳】EcoStar Sprint車はわずか9,999ドルの小売価格で、安く低排出の自動車を求めている消費者の間で人気を博している。

- □ popularly　㊄一般に　　　□ popularity　㊄人気　　　□ popularize　㊄普及する
- □ retail　㊄小売りする　　□ consumer　㊄消費者　　□ low-emission　㊄低排出の

11. 正解 (D)

【解説】addressは「～に向けて述べる；対処する」という意味の動詞で、これを修飾する部分が空所となっているので、副詞のsuitably（適切に）が適当。

構造 Professor Kalima's book, *Risks and Opportunities* ⓢ, (suitably) addresses ⓥ emerging forces ⟨in the global farming sector⟩.

【訳】Kalima教授の著書『リスクと機会』は世界の農業分野における新興勢力について適切に考察している。

- □ suited　suitの過去(分詞)形　　□ suiting　suitの現在分詞形　　□ suit　㊄適する
- □ emerging　㊄新興の　　　　　□ farming　㊄農業

12. 正解 (D)

【解説】present（発表する）という他動詞の目的語となり、またinsightful（洞察力に満ちた）という形容詞に修飾されている部分なので、名詞のanalyses（analysis〈分析〉の複数形）が適当。

構造 Chief Financial Officer John Xiu ⓢ presented ⓥ some insightful analyses ⓞ ⟨of the company's cash position⟩ (at the board meeting).

【訳】最高財務責任者のJohn Xiuは取締役会議において、会社の財務状況に関していくつかの洞察力に富む分析結果を発表した。

- □ analyzes　　　　　　㊄分析する　　　□ analytically　㊄分析的に　　□ analyst　㊄分析者
- □ Chief Financial Officer　㊄最高財務責任者　□ cash position　㊄財務状況　□ board meeting　㊄取締役会議

13. The Azumi Electric Knife cuts ------- well through fish, chicken or even frozen meats.
   (A) remarkably
   (B) remark
   (C) remarking
   (D) remarks

14. Ms. Wang brings ------- expertise to her writings for Money Street Magazine, since she was a fund manager for many years.
   (A) authorize
   (B) authority
   (C) authoritative
   (D) authorizing

15. Municipal authorities have been ------- persuasive in convincing small business owners to relocate into the city.
   (A) surprisingly
   (B) surprising
   (C) surprised
   (D) surprises

16. Aromacof Café invested €2.3 million in coffee-growing farmland in Kenya, the maximum ------- under its current budget.
   (A) permits
   (B) permissible
   (C) permissive
   (D) permissibly

13. 正解 (A)
【解説】well という副詞を修飾する部分に空所があるので、副詞の remarkably (著しく) が適当。これは形容詞の remarkable (著しい) に接尾辞の -ly が付いて副詞になったもの。

構造 The Azumi Electric Knife ⓢ cuts ⓥ (remarkably well) (through fish, chicken or even frozen meats).

【訳】Azumi電動ナイフは魚肉、チキンから冷凍肉にいたるまでたいへんよく切れる。

- □ remark ⓥ述べる
- □ remarking　remark の現在分詞形
- □ remarks ⓝ意見

14. 正解 (C)
【解説】expertise は「専門知識」という名詞。それを修飾する部分が空所となっているので、形容詞の authoritative (権威ある) を選べばよい。-ive は主に形容詞を作る接尾辞。

構造 Ms. Wang ⓢ brings ⓥ authoritative expertise ⓞ (to her writings ⟨for Money Street Magazine⟩), (since she was a fund manager (for many years)).

【訳】Wang氏は、長年ファンドマネジャーを勤めていたため、Money Street Magazineの記事には権威ある専門知識が加えられている。

- □ authorize ⓥ権限を与える
- □ authority ⓝ権威
- □ authorizing　authorize の現在分詞形
- □ fund ⓝ資金；国債

15. 正解 (A)
【解説】persuasive (説得力のある) という形容詞を修飾する部分に空所があるため、副詞の surprisingly (驚くほどに) が適当。これは surprise (驚かせる) という動詞が現在分詞となり形容詞化した surprising (驚くべき) に、接尾辞の -ly が付いて副詞となったもの。

構造 Municipal authorities ⓢ have been ⓥ (surprisingly) persuasive ⓒ (in [convincing small business owners to relocate (into the city)]).

【訳】市当局は驚くほどの説得力をもって小規模自営業者の市内への移転を促してきた。

- □ surprising ⓐ驚くべき
- □ surprised ⓐ驚いた
- □ surprises ⓥ驚かす
- □ municipal authorities ⓝ市当局
- □ convince ~ to V ⓘ~を説得してVさせる
- □ relocate ⓥ移転させる

16. 正解 (B)
【解説】the maximum という名詞の前のカンマは €2.3 million という額を同格的に言い換える働きをしている。空所以下はこの maximum という名詞を後ろから修飾する働きをするので形容詞 permissible (許容できる) が入る。permissive (寛大な) も形容詞だが、文意に合わない。

構造 Aromacof Café ⓢ invested ⓥ €2.3 million ⓞ, (in coffee-growing farmland ⟨in Kenya⟩), the maximum permissible ⟨under its current budget⟩.

【訳】Aromacof Café 社は230万ユーロをケニアのコーヒー農園に投資したが、これは現在の予算の範囲内で許容できる最大限の額であった。

- □ permits ⓥ許可する
- □ permissive ⓐ寛大な
- □ permissibly ⓐ差し支えない程度に
- □ invest ⓥ投資する
- □ current ⓐ現在の
- □ budget ⓝ予算

17. The revolutionary design of the Larpesky Washing Machine ------- reduces the washing cycle for a normal load to just ten minutes.
   (A) essential
   (B) essence
   (C) essentially
   (D) essentialist   Ⓐ Ⓑ Ⓒ Ⓓ

18. It took two years from the initial ------- phases of the RT9000 commercial airplane to its mass production.
   (A) developers
   (B) development
   (C) developmentally
   (D) develop   Ⓐ Ⓑ Ⓒ Ⓓ

19. The Harper Mining Corporation CEO ------- denied media reports that he was preparing to resign.
   (A) aggression
   (B) aggressively
   (C) aggressor
   (D) aggressive   Ⓐ Ⓑ Ⓒ Ⓓ

20. Consuela Advertising ------ hires models for its commercials based on how their images enhance certain products or services.
   (A) selecting
   (B) selection
   (C) selectively
   (D) selective   Ⓐ Ⓑ Ⓒ Ⓓ

17. 正解 (C)

【解説】reduce（減少させる）という動詞を修飾している部分なので、副詞のessentially（本質的に）が適当。これは、essential（根本的な）という形容詞に接尾辞の-lyが付いたもの。

構造 The revolutionary design ⓢ 〈of the Larpesky Washing Machine〉(essentially) reduces ⓥ the washing cycle ⓞ 〈for a normal load〉(to just ten minutes).

【訳】Larpesky洗濯機の革新的な設計により、通常の洗濯量であれば、洗濯サイクルをわずか10分に、根本的に減少させることができる。

- ☐ essential　㊝根本的な
- ☐ essence　㊅本質
- ☐ essentialist　㊅本質主義者
- ☐ revolutionary　㊝革新的な
- ☐ load　㊅仕事量

18. 正解 (B)

【解説】phases（段階）という名詞を修飾する部分に空所があるが、選択肢には形容詞はない。これは、名詞が直後の名詞を修飾し2語の句を作る用法。名詞development（開発）と繋げてdevelopment phase「開発段階」という名詞句になる。-mentは名詞を作る接尾辞。

構造 It ⓢ took ⓥ two years ⓞ (from the initial development phases 〈of the RT9000 commercial airplane〉)(to its mass production).

【訳】RT9000商用機の初期開発段階から、その量産へと至るには、2年の歳月を要した。

- ☐ developers　㊅開発者
- ☐ developmentally　㊙発展的に
- ☐ develop　㊙発達させる
- ☐ initial　㊝最初の
- ☐ commercial　㊝商業上の
- ☐ mass production　㊅大量生産

19. 正解 (B)

【解説】動詞deny（否定する）を修飾する部分が空所なので、副詞のaggressively（攻撃的に）が適当。これはaggressive（攻撃的な）という形容詞に、-lyという接尾辞が付き副詞となったもの。

構造 The Harper Mining Corporation CEO ⓢ (aggressively) denied ⓥ media reports ⓞ 〈that he was preparing to resign〉.

【訳】Harper Mining社のCEOは彼が辞職の準備をしているというメディアのレポートを激しく否定した。

- ☐ aggression　㊅攻撃
- ☐ aggressor　㊅攻撃者
- ☐ aggressive　㊝攻撃的な
- ☐ corporation　㊅企業；会社
- ☐ prepare　㊙準備する
- ☐ resign　㊙辞職する

20. 正解 (C)

【解説】hire（雇う）という動詞を修飾する部分なので、副詞のselectively（選択して）が適当。これはselective（選択の）という形容詞に接尾辞の-lyが付いて副詞となったもの。

構造 Consuela Advertising ⓢ (selectively) hires ⓥ models ⓞ 〈for its commercials〉(based on [how their images enhance certain products or services]).

【訳】Consuela Advertising社はそのモデルのイメージがある種の製品やサービスの価値をいかに高めるかを基準にコマーシャル用のモデルを雇っている。

- ☐ selecting　selectの現在分詞形
- ☐ selection　㊅選択
- ☐ selective　㊝選択の
- ☐ hire　㊙雇う
- ☐ enhance　㊙高める
- ☐ certain　㊝ある

21. Mr. Redstone implemented a more ------- management style, taking a long-term view on all the company's products.
  (A) strategy
  (B) strategic
  (C) strategize
  (D) strategically

22. Ackton Inc. will hold a special seminar on May 9 for personnel to receive ------- training on the new software systems.
  (A) introduce
  (B) introductions
  (C) introducing
  (D) introductory

23. Inter-Face Consulting teaches corporations to be culturally ------- when designing their overseas advertisements.
  (A) sensitively
  (B) sensitivity
  (C) sensitive
  (D) sensitize

24. After numerous revisions, the new ------- for Upside, a new line of suits for men, was finally broadcast yesterday.
  (A) commercialize
  (B) commercially
  (C) commercial
  (D) commerce

21. 正解 (B)

【解説】空所は management style（経営方式）という名詞句を修飾する部分なので、形容詞の strategic（戦略的な）を入れればよい。-ic は主に形容詞を作る接尾辞。

構造 Mr. Redstone ⓢ implemented ⓥ a more strategic management style ⓞ, (taking a long-term view (on all the company's products)).

【訳】Redstone 氏は、会社のすべての製品に対して長期的な見通しを持ち、より戦略的な経営方式を実践した。

- ☐ strategy ⓝ戦略
- ☐ strategize ⓥ作戦を練る
- ☐ strategically ⓐ戦略的に
- ☐ implement ⓥ実行する
- ☐ long-term ⓐ長期の
- ☐ view ⓝ見通し

22. 正解 (D)

【解説】training（トレーニング）という名詞を修飾する部分に空所があるので、形容詞の introductory（入門的な）を選ぶ。

構造 Ackton Inc. ⓢ will hold ⓥ a special seminar ⓞ (on May 9) ⟨for personnel to receive introductory training ⟨on the new software systems⟩⟩.

【訳】Ackton 社は、全社員が新しいソフトウェアシステムの入門的トレーニングを受けることができるセミナーを5月9日に開催する。

- ☐ introduce ⓥ紹介する
- ☐ introductions ⓝ紹介
- ☐ introducing introduce の現在分詞形
- ☐ personnel ⓝ全職員
- ☐ receive ⓥ受け取る；受ける

23. 正解 (C)

【解説】corporations（会社）を意味上の主語とし、be 動詞の補語となる部分なので sensitive（敏感な）という形容詞を選ぶ。culturally（文化的に）という副詞は sensitive を修飾している。

構造 Inter-Face Consulting ⓢ teaches ⓥ corporations ⓞ to be culturally sensitive (when designing their overseas advertisements).

【訳】Inter-Face Consulting は、海外の宣伝を企画する際には、文化的な配慮をするように、企業を指導している。

- ☐ sensitively ⓐ敏感に
- ☐ sensitivity ⓝ感受性
- ☐ sensitize ⓥ敏感になる
- ☐ overseas ⓐ海外の
- ☐ advertisement ⓝ宣伝；広告

24. 正解 (C)

【解説】new という形容詞の直後に空所があるので名詞を入れるのが適当。commerce も名詞だがこれは「商業」という意味で文意に合わないので、commercial（宣伝番組）を選ぶ。

構造 (After numerous revisions), the new commercial ⓢ ⟨for Upside, a new line of suits for men⟩, was (finally) broadcast ⓥ (yesterday).

【訳】何度も修正をした後、男性用スーツの新製品、Upside の新しいコマーシャルは昨日ついに放送された。

- ☐ commercialize ⓥ商品化する
- ☐ commercially ⓐ営利的に
- ☐ commerce ⓝ商業
- ☐ numerous ⓐたくさんの
- ☐ revision ⓝ修正
- ☐ line ⓝ品ぞろえ

25. The rise of Hong Kong as a major financial city had ------- growth effects on the entire Pacific Rim economy.
   (A) intend
   (B) intensive
   (C) intention
   (D) intensively

26. Call center staff are prohibited from using their desk telephones for anything but company matters, except in cases of ------ emergencies.
   (A) personality
   (B) personalizing
   (C) person
   (D) personal

27. The regional manager was always ------ when inspecting local stores, so she could get a genuine idea of how they were performing.
   (A) objective
   (B) object
   (C) objectively
   (D) objection

28. Scientists at Daweed Chemicals Inc. had ------- tested the new material until it was proven to meet their standards.
   (A) repetition
   (B) repeatedly
   (C) repetitive
   (D) repeating

25. 正解 (B)

【解説】growth effect は「成長を促す影響」という意味の名詞句。これを修飾する形容詞の intensive（激しい；集中的な）を選ぶ。

構造 The rise (S) ⟨of Hong Kong⟩ ⟨as a major financial city⟩ had (V) intensive growth effects (O) ⟨on the entire Pacific Rim economy⟩.

【訳】主要な金融都市としての香港の興隆は、環太平洋地域全体の経済に対して劇的な影響を与えた。

- □ intend　動 意図する
- □ rise　名 隆盛；向上；上昇；増加
- □ Pacific Rim　名 環太平洋地域
- □ intention　名 意図
- □ financial　形 金融上の
- □ economy　名 経済
- □ intensively　動 激しく
- □ entire　形 全体の

26. 正解 (D)

【解説】emergency（緊急事態）という名詞を修飾する部分なので、形容詞の personal（個人的な）を選ぶ。

構造 Call center staff (S) are prohibited (V) ⟨from using their desk telephones ⟨for anything ⟨but company matters⟩⟩⟩, ⟨except in cases of personal emergencies⟩.

【訳】コールセンターの職員は、個人的な緊急事態の場合を除き、会社関連以外の用事で卓上の電話を使うことを禁じられている。

- □ personality　名 個性
- □ prohibit ~ from Ving　熟 ~がVするのを禁止する
- □ personalizing　personalize の現在分詞形
- □ in cases of ~　熟 ~の場合には
- □ person　名 人

27. 正解 (A)

【解説】第2文型の英文。the regional manager（地区責任者）を主語とし、was という be 動詞の補語にあたる部分が空所なので、文意に適した形容詞の objective（客観的な）が正解。

構造 The regional manager (S) was (V) ⟨always⟩ objective (C) ⟨when inspecting local stores⟩, so she (S) could get (V) a genuine idea (O) ⟨of [how they were performing]⟩.

【訳】地区責任者は、店舗の営業の様子を正確に把握するため、地域の店舗を視察する際には常に客観性を保っていた。

- □ object　動 反対する
- □ inspect　動 視察する
- □ objectively　副 客観的に
- □ genuine　形 真の
- □ objection　名 反対
- □ perform　動 行う

28. 正解 (B)

【解説】test（試験する）という動詞を修飾する部分が空所なので、副詞 repeatedly（繰り返して）を選択する。これは repeated（たびたびの）という形容詞に接尾辞 -ly が付き副詞となったもの。

構造 Scientists (S) ⟨at Daweed Chemicals Inc.⟩ had ⟨repeatedly⟩ tested (V) the new material (O) ⟨until it was proven to meet their standards⟩.

【訳】Daweed Chemicals 社の科学者は、新素材が基準値を満たすと証明できるまで、繰り返しその素材を試験し続けた。

- □ repetition　名 繰り返し
- □ material　名 素材；資料
- □ repetitive　形 繰り返しの
- □ prove　動 証明する
- □ repeating　repeat の現在分詞形
- □ standard　名 基準

文型に即した品詞の選択

29. The new Superspeed broadband package allows Internet users to ------- search an unlimited number of Web sites.
(A) optimally
(B) optimize
(C) optimal
(D) optimizer

Ⓐ Ⓑ Ⓒ Ⓓ

30. As part of its ------ marking 20 years of business, the Maple Leaf Boutique offers customers a 10% discount on nearly all items in the store.
(A) celebration
(B) celebrate
(C) celebratory
(D) celebrated

Ⓐ Ⓑ Ⓒ Ⓓ

31. Myro Corporation focuses on ------- in staff training to generate substantially high increases in its productivity rate.
(A) invests
(B) investor
(C) invested
(D) investment

Ⓐ Ⓑ Ⓒ Ⓓ

32. Assembly line employees were asked to work extra shifts in order to make sure ------- client orders were met.
(A) addition
(B) add
(C) adding
(D) additional

Ⓐ Ⓑ Ⓒ Ⓓ

29. 正解 （A）

【解説】search（探す）という動詞を修飾する部分なので、副詞のoptimally（最適に）が適当。これは、形容詞のoptimal（最適な）に、接尾辞の-lyが付いて副詞となったもの。

構造 The new Superspeed broadband package ⓢ allows ⓥ Internet users ⓞ to optimally search an unlimited number of Web sites ⓒ.

【訳】新しいSuperspeedブロードバンドパッケージを使えば、インターネットのユーザーは最適な方法でウェブサイトを無制限に検索することができる。

- □ optimize 動最大限に利用する
- □ optimal 形最適な
- □ optimizer 名最適化するもの

30. 正解 （A）

【解説】ofという前置詞の目的語になっていること、直前にitsという代名詞の所有格があることから、名詞celebration（祝典）が適当。-tionは名詞を作る接尾辞。markingからbusinessまではこの名詞を修飾する形容詞句。

構造 (As part of its celebration ⟨marking 20 years of business⟩), the Maple Leaf Boutique ⓢ offers ⓥ customers ⓞ₁ a 10% discount ⓞ₂ ⟨on nearly all items⟩ ⟨in the store⟩.

【訳】開業20周年記念の一環として、the Maple Leaf Boutiqueは店内のほとんどすべての商品に関して、10%の割引を顧客に提供する。

- □ celebrate 動祝う
- □ celebratory 形祝賀の
- □ celebrated celebrateの過去（分詞）形
- □ as part of〜 熟〜の一環として
- □ mark 動示す
- □ customer 名顧客

31. 正解 （D）

【解説】onという前置詞の目的語となる部分が空所なので、名詞investment（投資）が適当。-mentは名詞を作る接尾辞。

構造 Myro Corporation ⓢ focuses ⓥ ⟨on investment⟩ ⟨in staff training⟩ ⟨to generate substantially high increases⟨in its productivity rate⟩⟩.

【訳】Myro社はその極めて高い生産性向上率を生み出すために、社員研修への投資を重視している。

- □ invests 動投資する
- □ investor 名投資家
- □ invested investの過去（分詞）形
- □ focus on 熟〜に焦点を合わせる
- □ staff training 名社員研修
- □ generate 動生み出す
- □ substantially 副相当に
- □ productivity 名生産性

32. 正解 （D）

【解説】client orders（顧客の注文）という名詞句を修飾する部分なので、形容詞のadditional（追加の）を選ぶ。

構造 Assembly line employees ⓢ were asked ⓥ to work extra shifts (in order to make sure [additional client orders were met]).

【訳】流れ作業に従事する職員は、顧客の追加注文を確実に完了するために、追加勤務をするように求められた。

- □ addition 名追加
- □ add 動加える
- □ adding addの現在分詞形
- □ assembly line 名流れ作業
- □ employee 名従業員
- □ shift 名勤務時間
- □ client 名顧客
- □ meet 動応じる

文型に即した品詞の選択

33. Super One Diet Cola has half the calories of Super One Cola, while maintaining the tasty ------- flavor only found in the Super One beverage brands.
(A) origin
(B) originating
(C) original
(D) originally

34. In spite of ------ losses incurred by Hani Seol Manufacturing Corp., CEO Kang Ju-young stated the company would experience a turnaround within two quarters.
(A) signify
(B) significantly
(C) significance
(D) significant

35. Profits at Xenon Electronics are rising ------- because of an upsurge in demand from younger consumers.
(A) sharp
(B) sharpness
(C) sharply
(D) sharpen

36. Mojem Office Art Inc. specializes in decorating building interiors with ------- pieces of modern art in and around the Greater New Delhi area.
(A) valuing
(B) values
(C) valuation
(D) valuable

33. 正解　(C)

【解説】flavor（風味）という名詞を修飾する部分に空所があるので、形容詞のoriginal（独特な）が正解。tasty（美味しい）という形容詞もflavorという名詞を修飾している。

構造 Super One Diet Cola ⓢ has ⓥ half the calories ⓞ ⟨of Super One Cola⟩, (while maintaining the tasty original flavor ⟨only found in the Super One beverage brands⟩).

【訳】Super Oneダイエットコーラのカロリーは Super Oneコーラの半分だが、Super Oneブランドの飲料だけが持つ美味しい独特の風味を残している。

- □ origin　名起源
- □ originating　originate の現在分詞形
- □ originally　副独創的に

34. 正解　(D)

【解説】losses（損失）という名詞を修飾している部分なので、形容詞significant（重大な）を選ぶ。

構造 (In spite of significant losses ⟨incurred (by Hani Seol Manufacturing Corp.,)⟩) CEO Kang Ju-young ⓢ stated ⓥ [ⓞ the company would experience a turnaround (within two quarters)].

【訳】Hani Seol Manufacturing社がこうむった重大な損失にもかかわらず、CEOのKang Ju-youngはこれから2四半期以内に、同社は業績の回復が見込めるであろうと述べた。

- □ signify　動意味する
- □ significantly　副意味ありげに
- □ significance　名重要性
- □ incur　動こうむる
- □ state　動はっきり述べる
- □ experience　動経験する
- □ turnaround　名転換；業績の好転
- □ quarter　名四半期

35. 正解　(C)

【解説】rise（増加する）という動詞を修飾している部分なので、副詞を選択する。sharpという形容詞に-lyという接尾辞が付き、副詞sharply（急に）となっている。

構造 Profits ⓢ ⟨at Xenon Electronics⟩ are rising ⓥ (sharply) (because of an upsurge ⟨in demand ⟨from younger consumers⟩⟩).

【訳】若い消費者の需要の増大により、Xenon Electronics社の利益は急激に増加している。

- □ sharp　形鋭い
- □ sharpness　名鋭さ
- □ sharpen　動鋭くする
- □ profit　名利益
- □ upsurge　名急増
- □ demand　名需要

36. 正解　(D)

【解説】名詞pieces（作品）を修飾する部分が空所なので、形容詞のvaluable（貴重な）を選ぶ。-ableは主に形容詞を作る接尾辞。

構造 Mojem Office Art Inc. ⓢ specializes ⓥ (in [decorating building interiors (with valuable pieces ⟨of modern art⟩) (in and around the Greater New Delhi area)]).

【訳】Mojem Office Art社は、広域ニューデリー圏とその周辺において、建物の内装を貴重な現代アートの作品で装飾することを専門としている。

- □ valuing　valueの現在分詞形
- □ values　動評価する
- □ valuation　名評価
- □ specialize in 〜　熟〜を専門にする
- □ the Greater New Delhi area　名広域ニューデリー圏

37. Children are ------- waiting for Hi Smile Candies' new cherry-flavored mints.
   (A) expectant
   (B) expect
   (C) expectantly
   (D) expecting

38. Morale among employees with children became ------- higher after the introduction of telecommuting and daycare facilities.
   (A) demonstrative
   (B) demonstrate
   (C) demonstrably
   (D) demonstrated

39. Blue Star Shipping Ltd. ------- offered Mr. Nguyen the post of Chief Financial Officer, subject to his being available from April 7.
   (A) condition
   (B) conditionally
   (C) conditioned
   (D) conditional

40. The CEO found Ms. Krishna's ------- for intensified outsourcing to Bangladesh very convincing.
   (A) argues
   (B) argumentative
   (C) argument
   (D) arguably

37. 正解 (C)

【解説】waitという動詞を修飾している部分が空所なので、副詞のexpectantly（期待して）が適当。これは形容詞のexpectant（期待している）に、接尾辞の-lyが付き副詞になったもの。

構造 Children (s) are (expectantly) waiting (v) 〈for Hi Smile Candies' new cherry-flavored mints〉.

【訳】子供たちはHi Smile Candy社の新しいチェリー味のミントを待ち望んでいる。

- □ expectant　形 期待している
- □ expect　動 予期する
- □ expecting　expectの現在分詞形

38. 正解 (C)

【解説】higherという形容詞を修飾する部分が空所なので、副詞のdemonstrably（明らかに）が適当。これは、形容詞のdemonstrable（明白な）に接尾辞の-lyが付き、副詞となったもの。

構造 Morale (s) 〈among employees 〈with children〉〉 became (v) (demonstrably) higher (c) 〈after the introduction 〈of telecommuting and daycare facilities〉〉.

【訳】在宅勤務と託児施設の導入後、子供を持つ従業員の士気は明白に向上した。

- □ demonstrative　形 例証的な
- □ demonstrate　動 論証する
- □ demonstrated　demonstrateの過去（分詞）形
- □ morale　名 士気
- □ introduction　名 導入
- □ telecommuting　名 在宅勤務
- □ daycare　名 保育
- □ facility　名 施設

39. 正解 (B)

【解説】動詞offer（申し出る）を修飾する部分が空所なので、副詞のconditionally（条件付きで）が適当。これは形容詞のconditional（条件付きの）に、接尾辞の-lyが付き、副詞となったもの。

構造 Blue Star Shipping Ltd. (s) (conditionally) offered (v) Mr. Nguyen (o1) the post (o2) 〈of Chief Financial Officer〉, 〈subject to [his being available from April 7]〉.

【訳】Blue Star Shipping社はNguyen氏に、4月7日から空席となる、最高財務責任者の職を条件付きで申し出た。

- □ condition　名 状態
- □ conditioned　conditionの過去（分詞）形
- □ conditional　形 条件付きの
- □ subject to ~　熟 ~を条件として
- □ available　形 手に入る

40. 正解 (C)

【解説】Ms. Krishuna'sという所有格の固有名詞が直前にあることから、argument（主張）という名詞が空所には適当であると考えられる。-mentは名詞を作る接尾辞。

構造 The CEO (s) found (v) Ms. Krishna's argument (o) 〈for intensified outsourcing to Bangladesh〉 very convincing (c).

【訳】CEOはバングラデシュに集中的に外注するというKrishna氏の主張には非常に説得力があると考えた。

- □ argues　動 主張する
- □ argumentative　形 理屈っぽい
- □ arguably　動 ほぼ間違いなく
- □ intensify　動 強める
- □ outsourcing　名 外部調達
- □ convincing　形 人を納得させる

Lesson 2 文型に適した代名詞・関係詞の選択
基礎知識と文法ルールを確認！

◆代名詞の選択◆

　代名詞の基礎知識と文型の判別ができれば難しくはありません。**長い英文の構造を速く正確に把握する力が決め手**です。人称代名詞の表を確認しましょう。

主格	所有格	目的格	所有代名詞	再帰代名詞
I	my	me	mine	myself
we	our	us	ours	ourselves
you	your	you	yours	yourself
he	his	him	his	himself
she	her	her	hers	herself
they	their	them	theirs	themselves

- **主格**：文の主語の部分で用いられる際の代名詞の形です。
- **所有格**：名詞の前に置かれ、「〜の」という意味で用いられる際の形です。
- **目的格**：他動詞や前置詞の目的語となる場合に使われる形です。
- **所有代名詞**：たとえば my bike（私の自転車）のような表現が繰り返された場合に、bike という名詞の反復を避けるために使われる代名詞です。
- **再帰代名詞**：その名の通り、自分が行う動作が自分に向けられ戻ってくるような場合に使われます。たとえば、He looked at himself in the mirror.（彼は鏡で自分を見た）という文では、彼が行う「見る」という動作は自分自身に向けられています。このような場合に「再帰代名詞」が用いられます。

例題：Mr. Black was told by his secretary that an amazing number of people visited ------- office building yesterday.

(A) they　　(B) their　　(C) them　　(D) theirs

正解　**(B)**

訳　ブラックさんは秘書から、昨日は非常に多くの人が彼らの会社の建物を訪れたと教えられた。

【解説】確かに他動詞の後ろでもあるのですが、空所の後ろには office building という名詞があることから、所有格の (B)their が最も適切だと判断できます。直前に他動詞の visited があるからといって、もしも、(C)them を入れてしまうと、office building が文とは孤立して意味をなさなくなってしまいます。visited の目的語はあくまでも office building です。

◆関係詞の選択◆

関係詞とは**名詞を後ろで修飾・説明する場合に使われるつなぎ言葉**のことです。修飾される名詞の種類や、後ろに続く要素によって、様々な関係詞を使い分けなければなりません。空所に関係詞を補充する場合のルールを確認しましょう。

◎主格の関係代名詞

| 先行詞が人 | who [that] | V |
| 先行詞が物 | which [that] | V |

例 **Mr. Wang is looking for a person who [that] is suitable for the position.**
（ワン氏はその地位に適した人を探している）

主格の関係代名詞は直後に動詞が置かれ、先行詞となる名詞を修飾します。また、この動詞の形は、先行詞に合わせて決定されます。この主格の関係代名詞は省略することはできません。

◎所有格の関係代名詞

先行詞が人・物　whose　所有物の名詞　V（S V φ）

例 **Ms. Davis is looking for a candidate whose computer skills are as good as hers.**
（デイビス氏はそのコンピュータの技能が彼女と同等の候補者を探している）

先行詞の所有物を形容し先行詞を説明することができるのが、所有格の関係代名詞です。この whose の直後には先行詞の所有物となる名詞が置かれ、以降に動詞や節が続きます。この関係代名詞は省略することはできません。

◎目的格の関係代名詞

先行詞が人	who(m) [that]	S	V	φ	※節の終わりの部分は他動詞や前置詞の目的語が欠けた不完全な形となる。
先行詞が物	which [that]	S	V	φ	

例
Mr. Brown finally found the document <u>that [which]</u> he had been searching his office for φ.
Mr. Brown finally found the document <u>for which</u> he had been searching his office.
(ブラウン氏はオフィスで探していた書類をついに発見した)

　目的格の関係代名詞の直後には節が続きますが、この節には特徴があります。それは、**必ず、目的語のない他動詞や前置詞で不完全に終わっている**ということです。この目的語が欠落した箇所に先行詞を入れると文が通じます。目的格の関係代名詞はこのような場合に用いるのです。
　who(m)やwhichは多くの場合省略されます。thatも省略することができます。
　節の末尾が**on**や**in**など、**前置詞で終わる場合には、この前置詞をwhomやwhichの前に移動し、on whomやin whichという形にすることもできます**。この形ではthatを使用することはできません。

◎関係副詞

時	when	S	V
場所	where	S	V
理由	why	S	V

例
Julie finally told me the reason <u>why</u> she had been absent from the office for such a long time.
(ジュリーは彼女が会社を大変長い間休んでいた理由をついに私に教えてくれた)

　関係副詞の直後には文の要素が完全にそろった節が続きます。たとえば、whereとwhichのように、関係副詞と関係代名詞が選択肢に共に存在する場合には、先行詞の意味だけで判別することはできず、**後続する節が完全か不完全かによって、どちらかを決定**しなければならないわけです。

> 例題：Mr. Cage wanted to check on the development of the construction by actually visiting the site ------- the building was being built.
> (A) who (B) where (C) which (D) when

正解 **(B)**

訳 ケイジ氏は建物が建造中の場所を実際に訪問することで、建設の進行状況を確認することを望んだ。

【解説】先行詞はthe siteという「場所」とも「物」ともとれる単語なので、後続する節が完全か不完全かによって(B)whereか(C)whichを選択します。ここでは後続する文は受動態として完全に成立しており、欠落する要素はないので、(B)が正解となります。後続する文が受動態として独立して成立する完全な文であるということがわかるためには、動詞や受動態の理解が前提となります。

◎関係代名詞whatと接続詞thatの判別

関係代名詞のwhatは先行詞を中に含み、**主格として直後に動詞を続けることも、目的格として直後に目的語の欠落した節を続けることもできます。**意味は「(Sが)Vすること[もの]」となります。一方、接続詞のthatは直後に完全に要素がそろった節が続き、「〜ということ」という意味になります。この二つは、意味は似ているものの、後に続く要素が異なります。また、whatは何か具体的な物や事柄を念頭に置き「こと；もの」という内容を意味する場合に使われますが、thatは単に「以下に続く事実」を名詞節としてまとめているにすぎません。

> 例題：Not many people agreed with ------- Mr. Wedge said to the participants at the conference, so he had no choice but to revise his plan.
> (A) what (B) that (C) which (D) whose

正解 **(A)**

訳 会議で参加者に対してウェッジ氏が述べたことに対してあまり多くの人は賛成しなかったので、彼は計画を変更せざるを得なかった。

【解説】先行詞がないことから、答えは(A)whatか(B)thatに絞れます。形式的には直後にsaidの目的語が欠落した節が続いていることからwhatとわかります。また、会議で単に語ったという事実に賛成することはありませんから、この文ではMr. Wedgeが語った内容が想起されているのだと考えることができ、この点からも(A)whatが答えだとわかるわけです。

EXERCISES

空所補充：各文を完全な形にするために、必要な語句を1つだけ選んでください。

1. Best Meal Restaurants understands ------- diners are often too busy to spend long hours cooking.
   (A) it
   (B) they
   (C) its
   (D) theirs

2. Mr. Waleed ------- is planning to visit the new electronics factory later in the year.
   (A) himself
   (B) him
   (C) he
   (D) his

3. Mr. Park located the file ------- he wanted on his colleague's desk.
   (A) what
   (B) that
   (C) whose
   (D) when

4. The Madison Port Bridge finally reopened following reinforcements to ------- columns by Wang Min Corporation.
   (A) it's
   (B) its
   (C) which
   (D) their

全部で40問あります。1問20秒、13分20秒での完答を目指して挑戦しましょう。
すべて解答してから＜正解と解説＞と照合してください。

1. 正解 (C)

【解説】名詞diners（食事をする人）を修飾する部分が空所なので、所有格のitsが正解となる。このitsは主語のBest Meal Restaurantsを指している。

構造 Best Meal Restaurants ⓢ understands ⓥ [ₒ its diners are (often) too busy (to spend long hours cooking)].

【訳】Best Mealレストランは、そこで食事をする客はたいてい大変急いでいて、料理に時間がかけられないということを理解している。

□ spend 時間 (in) Ving 熟 Vするのに時間を使う　　□ diner 名 食事する人

2. 正解 (A)

【解説】「自分自身が」という意味を強調するために、主語などの直後に同格的に再帰代名詞が置かれることがある。ここでは、主語のMr. Waleed自身がということ。

構造 Mr. Waleed himself ⓢ is planning ⓥ [ₒ to visit the new electronics factory (later in the year)].

【訳】Waleed氏は自ら、今年後半に新しい電子機器工場を訪問する予定である。

□ later in the year 熟 今年後半に

3. 正解 (B)

【解説】空所の直後にはwantという動詞の目的語がない不完全な文が続いていることから、関係代名詞の目的格thatが適当。

構造 Mr. Park ⓢ located ⓥ the file ₒ ⟨that he wanted⟩ (on his colleague's desk).

【訳】Park氏は求めていたファイルを同僚の机の上に発見した。

□ locate 動 探し出す

4. 正解 (B)

【解説】column（橋脚）は橋に属する物なので、空所にはthe Madison Port Bridgeを指し、さらにcolumnを修飾する所有格のitsが入る。it'sは it is または it has の短縮形で所有格ではない。

構造 The Madison Port Bridge ⓢ (finally) reopened ⓥ (following reinforcements ⟨to its columns⟩ ⟨by Wang Min Corporation⟩).

【訳】Wang Min社による橋脚の補強を終え、Madison Port橋はついに再び開通した。

□ reopen 動 再開する　　□ reinforcement 名 補強

文型に適した代名詞・関係詞の選択

5. The Minsk City Activity Center has been specially designed for small children and ------- safety needs.
   (A) their
   (B) those
   (C) that
   (D) theirs

6. This secure, automated system lets callers enter payment details -------, rather than relying on staff.
   (A) them
   (B) they
   (C) theirs
   (D) themselves

7. The CEO contacted Professor Zhou, ------- opinion he valued on international buyouts.
   (A) his
   (B) their
   (C) whose
   (D) where

8. Gatanga Staffing Group built ------ reputation on helping corporations to find the best employees.
   (A) its
   (B) whose
   (C) which
   (D) those

5. 正解　(A)

【解説】空所がsafety needs（安全の必要性）という名詞句を修飾する部分にあることと、意味の上からsmall childrenを指していると考えられることから、この部分には所有格のtheirを入れるのが適当。

構造 The Minsk City Activity Center ⓢ has been (specially) designed ⓥ (for small children and their safety needs).

【訳】ミンスク市のアクティビティセンターは、特に幼児と彼らの安全の必要性を目的に設計されたものである。

☐ design 　動設計する

6. 正解　(D)

【解説】「自分自身で」ということを強調するために、強調する語の直後や動詞句の終わりに、まるで副詞のように、再帰代名詞が置かれることがある。ここでは、callers（電話をかける人たち）が「自分自身で」ということを強調するために、themselvesが用いられている。

構造 This secure, automated system ⓢ lets ⓥ callers ⓞ enter payment details themselves ⓒ, (rather than relying on staff).

【訳】この安全で自動化されたシステムを使えば、通話者はスタッフに頼らなくとも、支払いの詳細を自分で入力することができる。

☐ secure　形安全な　　　　☐ automated　形自動化された　　　☐ enter　動入力する
☐ detail　名詳細

7. 正解　(C)

【解説】空所の直後には、先行詞のProfessor Zhouに付帯する名詞、つまり所有物であるopinion（意見）があり、それが説明されていることから、関係代名詞の所有格whoseが適当。

構造 The CEO ⓢ contacted ⓥ Professor Zhou ⓞ, 〈whose opinion he valued (on international buyouts)〉.

【訳】CEOは、国際企業買収に関してその意見を尊重している、Zhou教授に連絡をとった。

☐ professor　名教授　　　☐ value　動尊重する　　　☐ buyout　名買収

8. 正解　(A)

【解説】空所がreputation（名声）という名詞を修飾する箇所にあるため、所有格の代名詞itsが適当。先行詞となるものがないため、関係代名詞は入らない。

構造 Gatanga Staffing Group ⓢ built ⓥ its reputation ⓞ (on [helping corporations to find the best employees]).

【訳】Gatanga Staffing Groupは、企業が最高の従業員を探す手助けをすることで、その名声を築いた。

9. Visitors to the park ------- litter in any way may be subject to a €200 fine.
   (A) their
   (B) what
   (C) who
   (D) where

   Ⓐ Ⓑ Ⓒ Ⓓ

10. Staff who cannot attend meetings must e-mail ------- reasons why 24 hours before such meetings start.
   (A) its
   (B) what
   (C) their
   (D) that

   Ⓐ Ⓑ Ⓒ Ⓓ

11. Membership programs for shoppers encourage ------- to make frequent purchase at the same location or facility.
   (A) themselves
   (B) them
   (C) him
   (D) his

   Ⓐ Ⓑ Ⓒ Ⓓ

12. If the user manual appears complex, refer to the pages ------- directly deal with your problem.
   (A) what
   (B) they
   (C) who
   (D) which

   Ⓐ Ⓑ Ⓒ Ⓓ

9. 正解 (C)

【解説】先行詞は visitors (訪問者) という人を表す言葉で、直後には litter (ゴミを散らかす) という動詞が続いているので、関係代名詞の主格の who が適当。the park は litter という動詞の主語には意味的になり得ないので、先行詞とは解釈できない。

【構造】 Visitors _(S) ⟨to the park⟩ ⟨who litter (in any way)⟩ may be _(V) subject _(C) (to a €200 fine).

【訳】いかなる形であろうと、ゴミを捨てた公園への来客は、200ユーロの罰金を払わなければならない。

□ be subject to 〜　(熟) 〜に従わなければならない　　□ fine　(名) 罰金

10. 正解 (C)

【解説】reasons why は「その理由」という意味の名詞句、それを修飾する箇所なので、所有格が適当。「職員」という意味の staff は個々の構成員を表す意味の場合は複数扱いをする。したがってここでは、their を用いるのがよい。

【構造】 Staff _(S) ⟨who cannot attend meetings⟩ must e-mail _(V) their reasons why _(O) (24 hours before such meetings start).

【訳】会合に出席することができない職員は、その理由を、その会合が始まる24時間前までにEメールで知らせなければならない。

□ attend　(動) 出席する　　□ meeting　(名) 会合　　□ e-mail　(動) 電子メールを送る

11. 正解 (B)

【解説】空所に入る代名詞は文の意味から、shoppers を指していると考えられるが、encourage (その気にさせる) という他動詞の目的語となっているため、目的格の them が適当。

【構造】 Membership programs _(S) ⟨for shoppers⟩ encourage _(V) them _(O) to make frequent purchase _(C) (at the same location or facility).

【訳】買い物客向けの会員プログラムにより、彼らは同じ場所や施設で買い物をしたい気持ちになる。

□ membership　(名) 会員　　□ shopper　(名) 買い物客　　□ encourage　(動) その気にさせる；奨励する
□ frequent　(形) 頻繁な　　□ make a purchase　(熟) 買い物をする

12. 正解 (D)

【解説】先行詞は the pages、空所の直後の directly という副詞をとばすと、動詞句の deal with..... (.....を扱う) が続いていることから、関係代名詞の主格が適当。

【構造】 (If the user manual appears complex), refer _(V) (to the pages ⟨which (directly) deal (with your problem)⟩).

【訳】使用者マニュアルが複雑に思える場合、問題を直接取り扱っているページを参照してください。

□ appear (to be) C　(熟) Cのように見える　　□ complex　(形) 複雑な　　□ refer to 〜　(熟) 〜を参照する

13. Data entry clerks ------ work with computers must rest their eyes from looking at monitors every few minutes.
   (A) what
   (B) where
   (C) when
   (D) who

14. Passengers are asked to fill in landing cards with their personal details with the pen ------ is provided.
   (A) when
   (B) that
   (C) why
   (D) what

15. Marketers know that by ------- a consumer survey offers limited information, but it is nevertheless important.
   (A) oneself
   (B) one's
   (C) it
   (D) itself

16. Mr. Greenburg thought more automation was ------- the factory needed to be more productive.
   (A) who
   (B) what
   (C) where
   (D) that

13. 正解 (D)

【解説】先行詞は人間を表す言葉で、空所の直後には動詞が続いていることから、関係代名詞の主格のwhoが適当。

構造 Data entry clerks (s) ⟨who work (with computers)⟩ must rest (v) their eyes (o) (from looking at monitors) (every few minutes).

【訳】コンピュータを使用しているデータ入力者は、数分おきにモニターを見ずに目を休めなければならない。

□ data entry clerk 名データ入力作業者　　□ monitor 名モニター

14. 正解 (B)

【解説】先行詞は the pen という物を表す言葉で、空所の直後には動詞が続いているため、関係代名詞の主格 that が適当。

構造 Passengers (s) are asked (v) to fill in landing cards (with their personal details) (with the pen ⟨that is provided⟩).

【訳】乗客は与えられたペンで、入国カードに個人情報を記入するように求められる。

□ fill in 熟記入する　　□ landing card 名入国カード　　□ personal details 名個人情報
□ provide 動与える；提供する

15. 正解 (D)

【解説】by itself は「単独で；それだけで(は)」という意味の再帰代名詞を用いたイディオム。全体で副詞句として用いる。

構造 Marketers (s) know (v) [(o) that (by itself) a consumer survey offers limited information, but it (s) is (v) (nevertheless) important (c)].

【訳】消費者調査は単独では限定された情報しか提供しないものの、それにもかかわらず重大であるということをマーケティング担当者は理解している。

□ marketer 名マーケティング担当者　　□ survey 名調査　　□ nevertheless 副それにもかかわらず

16. 正解 (B)

【解説】空所の直前には先行詞がなく、直後には need という他動詞の目的語がない不完全な文が続いていることから、関係代名詞の what が適当。

構造 Mr. Greenburg (s) thought (v) [(o) more automation was [what the factory needed (to be more productive)]].

【訳】Greenburg 氏は、工場の生産性をさらに高めるために必要なのはさらなるオートメーションであると考えた。

□ automation 名オートメーション　　□ productive 形生産的な

17. Lucy Dong stated that the company's global re-branding would be ------- department's main priority in the coming months.
   (A) she
   (B) theirs
   (C) her
   (D) hers

18. Sales representatives ------- want to change window displays must first gain approval from store managers.
   (A) who
   (B) where
   (C) what
   (D) when

19. The IT technician called Anna Ling in Human Resources, ------- computer he had been fixing earlier in the day.
   (A) who
   (B) that
   (C) which
   (D) whose

20. The Sunto Voicemail Service allows ------- to access messages from your laptop, cell phone or PDA.
   (A) you
   (B) yourself
   (C) your
   (D) yours

17. 正解 (C)

【解説】department（部門）という名詞を修飾する箇所に空所があるため、所有格のherが適当。

構造 Lucy Dong(s) stated(v) [(o)that the company's global re-branding would be her department's main priority (in the coming months)].

【訳】Lucy Dongは、社の世界的再ブランド化が、これからの数ヶ月において彼女の部門における最重要課題であると述べた。

- □ state 動言明する
- □ re-brand 動企業のイメージを変える
- □ priority 名優先事項

18. 正解 (A)

【解説】先行詞が人を表す名詞で、空所の直後には動詞が続いていることから、関係代名詞の主格のwhoが適当。

構造 Sales representatives(s) ⟨who want to change window displays⟩ must (first) gain(v) approval(o) ⟨from store managers⟩.

【訳】ウインドウディスプレイを変えようと望む販売員は、まず最初に店長からの承諾を得なければならない。

- □ gain 動得る
- □ approval 名承認

19. 正解 (D)

【解説】先行詞はAnna Lingという固有名詞、このような場合は関係詞の前にカンマのある非制限用法となる。空所の直後には、先行詞の所有物であるcomputerという名詞があり説明されているので、所有格のwhoseが適当。

構造 The IT technician(s) called(v) Anna Ling(o) ⟨in Human Resources⟩, ⟨whose computer he had been fixing (earlier in the day)⟩.

【訳】IT技師は人事部のAnna Ling氏に電話をしたが、彼は彼女のコンピュータをその日早くから修理していた。

- □ technician 名技術者
- □ human resources 名人事部

20. 正解 (A)

【解説】一般的な人を表す場合にはyouという代名詞を用いる。ここではallowの目的語となっているため、目的格のyouが適当。

構造 The Sunto Voicemail Service(s) allows(v) you(o) to access messages(c) (from your laptop, cell phone or PDA).

【訳】Sunto社のボイスメールサービスにより、ノートパソコンや携帯電話やPDAから、メッセージにアクセスできるようになる。

- □ laptop 名ノートパソコン
- □ cell phone 名携帯電話
- □ PDA 名personal digital assistantの略。携帯用コンピュータ

21. The warehouse supervisor instructed workers not to touch the radios ------- had been damaged in transit.
  (A) theirs
  (B) which
  (C) whose
  (D) where

22. Sales assistants with cell phones are no longer allowed to bring ------- onto the store premises.
  (A) they
  (B) their
  (C) themselves
  (D) them

23. Chief Financial Officer Yu gives ------ feedback on production targets, based on the company's budget.
  (A) her
  (B) who
  (C) what
  (D) she

24. Director Itoh holds regular conferences with all managers ------ lead departments under him.
  (A) when
  (B) who
  (C) they
  (D) that

21. 正解 (B)

【解説】先行詞は the radios で空所の直後には動詞が続いていることから、関係代名詞の主格の which が適当。

構造 The warehouse supervisor ⓢ instructed ⓥ workers ⓞ not to touch the radios ⓞ 〈which had been damaged (in transit)〉.

【訳】倉庫の管理者は従業員に、運送過程で破損した無線機にはさわらないように指示した。

- □ warehouse ㊂倉庫
- □ supervisor ㊂上司；管理者
- □ instruct ㋺指示する
- □ transit ㊂運送

22. 正解 (D)

【解説】bring という他動詞の目的語となっているので、目的格の them が適当。これは cell phones を指している。

構造 Sales assistants ⓢ 〈with cell phones〉 are (no longer) allowed ⓥ to bring them (onto the store premises).

【訳】携帯電話を持った販売員は、それらを持って店の敷地に入ることはもはや許されない。

- □ sales assistant ㊂販売員
- □ no longer ㊛もはや.....ない

23. 正解 (A)

【解説】feedback は「意見；感想」という意味の名詞で、これを修飾する箇所に空所があるため、所有格の her が適当。この her は主語の Yu 氏を指している。

構造 Chief Financial Officer Yu ⓢ gives ⓥ, her feedback ⓞ 〈on production targets〉, (based on the company's budget).

【訳】最高財務責任者の Yu 氏は会社の予算に基づいて、生産目標に関しての彼女の意見を出している。

- □ production ㊂生産
- □ target ㊂目標

24. 正解 (B)

【解説】先行詞は all managers で、直後には lead という動詞が続いているため、関係代名詞の主格の who が適当。

構造 Director Itoh ⓢ holds ⓥ regular conferences ⓞ (with all managers 〈who lead departments under him〉).

【訳】取締役の Itoh 氏は、彼の下で部門を率いているすべての課長と定期的な会議を開く。

- □ director ㊂重役
- □ regular ㋳定期的な
- □ conference ㊂会議
- □ lead ㋺率いる
- □ department ㊂部門

25. Employees working for five or more hours are entitled to two 10-minute rest breaks, and may take ------- at any time.
    (A) their
    (B) them
    (C) it
    (D) us

26. The clerk called Ms. Chang to tell her the DVD ------- she had ordered was now in the store.
    (A) that
    (B) who
    (C) when
    (D) where

27. Greengrass Groceries Co. will close for three weeks for renovation, although ------- hopes to move that date up if possible.
    (A) it
    (B) that
    (C) which
    (D) those

28. Amber Thompson Co. raised ------- funds for the merger by borrowing from various banks.
    (A) itself
    (B) his
    (C) its
    (D) themselves

25. 正解 (B)

【解説】文の意味から、空所に入る代名詞はrest breaksを指すと考えられる。またtakeという他動詞の目的語となっていることから、目的格のthemが正解となる。

構造 Employees ⓢ 〈working for five or more hours〉 are entitled ⓥ1 (to two 10-minute rest breaks), and may take ⓥ2 them ⓞ (at any time).

【訳】5時間以上働く従業員には、10分間の休みを2度とる権利が与えられ、それらをいつでもとってもよい。

□be entitled to ~ 熟〜の権利がある　□rest break 名休憩時間　□at any time 熟いつでも

26. 正解 (A)

【解説】空所の直後には、orderという他動詞の目的語がない不完全な文が続いている。このような場合には関係代名詞の目的格のthatが適当。

構造 The clerk ⓢ called ⓥ Ms. Chang ⓞ (to tell her [the DVD 〈that she had ordered〉 was (now) (in the store)]).

【訳】店員はChang氏に彼女が注文していたDVDがもう店に届いていると告げるために電話をした。

□clerk 名店員

27. 正解 (A)

【解説】空所に入る部分はGreengrass Groceries Co.を指している。また、空所は主語の位置にあることから、主格の代名詞、itが正解となる。先行詞がないため、関係代名詞は使えない。

構造 Greengrass Groceries Co. ⓢ will close ⓥ (for three weeks) (for renovation), (although it hopes [to move that date up] (if possible)).

【訳】Greengrass食品社は、可能であれば期間を短縮したいものの、改装のため、3週間閉鎖する予定だ。

□close 動閉鎖する　□renovation 名改装　□move up 熟繰り上げる
□possible 形可能な

28. 正解 (C)

【解説】文の意味から、空所に入る代名詞はAmber Thompson Co.を指していると考えられる。また、直後のfunds（資金）という名詞を修飾していることから、所有格の代名詞itsが適当。

構造 Amber Thompson Co. ⓢ raised ⓥ its funds ⓞ 〈for the merger〉 (by borrowing (from various banks)).

【訳】Amber Thompson社は様々な銀行から借り入れをすることによって、合併のための資金を調達した。

□raise 動調達する；持ち上げる　□merger 名合併　□various 形様々な

文型に適した代名詞・関係詞の選択

29. Executives from the Stoddard Gold and Silver Company chartered a plane to fly over the area ------- they hoped to start mining.
  (A) what
  (B) whose
  (C) who
  (D) where Ⓐ Ⓑ Ⓒ Ⓓ

30. Mayor Singh said that lower subway fares, ------- have been in effect since last month, have increased ridership by 16%.
  (A) what
  (B) who
  (C) which
  (D) whose Ⓐ Ⓑ Ⓒ Ⓓ

31. Finance Director Leibowitz, ------- hard work helped win the Franklin contract, has been rewarded with a promotion.
  (A) who
  (B) that
  (C) where
  (D) whose Ⓐ Ⓑ Ⓒ Ⓓ

32. More and more Dublin stores are appealing to ------- core customers through discounts.
  (A) when
  (B) its
  (C) their
  (D) that Ⓐ Ⓑ Ⓒ Ⓓ

29. 正解 (D)

【解説】空所の直後には、要素がすべてそろった完全な文が置かれている。また、先行詞として the area(地域)という場所を表す名詞があるため、関係副詞の where が適当。

【構造】Executives ⓢ ⟨from the Stoddard Gold and Silver Company⟩ chartered ⓥ a plane ⓞ (to fly (over the area ⟨where they hoped to start mining⟩)).

【訳】Stoddard Gold and Silver社の重役は、採掘を始めたいと思っている地域の上を飛ぶために飛行機をチャーターした。

□ charter 動借り切る　　□ mine 動採掘する

30. 正解 (C)

【解説】lower subway fares(地下鉄の値下げ運賃)が先行詞で、空所の直後には動詞が続いていることから、関係代名詞の主格の which が適当。

【構造】Mayor Singh ⓢ said ⓥ [ₒ that lower subway fares, ⟨which have been in effect since last month⟩, have increased ridership (by 16%)].

【訳】Singh市長は、先月から施行された地下鉄の値下げ運賃によって、乗車率が16%上がったと述べた。

□ in effect 熟施行されている;有効な　　□ increase 動増える;増やす　　□ ridership 名乗車率

31. 正解 (D)

【解説】空所の直後に、先行詞に付帯する名詞が置かれており、その説明が続いていることから、関係代名詞の所有格の whose が適当。

【構造】Finance Director Leibowitz ⓢ, ⟨whose hard work helped win the Franklin contract⟩, has been rewarded ⓥ (with a promotion).

【訳】その勤労のおかげでFranklin社との契約を可能とした財務部長のLeibowitz氏は、昇進により報われることとなった。

□ finance 名財務;金融　　□ help (to) V 熟Vするのに役立つ　　□ win 動獲得する
□ contract 名契約　　□ reward 動報いる　　□ promotion 名昇進

32. 正解 (C)

【解説】core customers(固定客)という名詞を修飾する部分に空所があるので、所有格の their が適当。stores という名詞の複数形を指しているため、単数名詞を指す its は使えない。

【構造】More and more Dublin stores ⓢ are appealing ⓥ (to their core customers) (through discounts).

【訳】割引を通じて固定客を引きつけようとしているダブリンの商店がますます増えている。

□ more and more ~ 熟ますます多くの~　　□ appeal to ~ 熟~に訴える　　□ core 形主要な

33. Mr. Yanayev introduced Ms. Chow, to ------- he had referred earlier in his speech.
  (A) where
  (B) whom
  (C) that
  (D) her

34. Vice-president Li always trusts ------- division heads to keep informed of local market conditions.
  (A) her
  (B) that
  (C) their
  (D) hers

35. The new recruits finally had a chance to meet CEO Jaden Dominguez, ------- fame as a business leader they already knew.
  (A) who
  (B) whose
  (C) what
  (D) his

36. Black Tower Construction was pleased to find ------- finally won the rights to build the Golden Dragon Amusement Park in China.
  (A) themselves
  (B) itself
  (C) their
  (D) it

33. 正解 (B)

【解説】refer という動詞は refer to 〜という形で、「〜に言及する」という意味になる。ここでは、この to が目的格の関係代名詞 whom の直前に移動し、to whom という形になっている。

構造 Mr. Yanayev ⓢ introduced ⓥ Ms. Chow ⓞ, 〈to whom he had referred (earlier in his speech)〉.

【訳】Yanayev 氏はそのスピーチの中で先んじて彼が言及した、Chow 氏を紹介した。

□ introduce　⑩紹介する

34. 正解 (A)

【解説】division heads という名詞句を修飾する部分に空所があるため、Li 氏を指す所有格の代名詞 her が適当。

構造 Vice-president Li ⓢ (always) trusts ⓥ her division heads ⓞ to keep informed (of local market conditions).

【訳】副社長の Li 氏は地域の市場の状況を把握することにおいて、彼女の下で働く部長たちを常に信頼している。

□ vice-president　⑧副社長　　□ trust　⑩信頼する　　□ division　⑧部門
□ informed　⑱知識のある　　□ market　⑧市場　　□ condition　⑧状況；条件

35. 正解 (B)

【解説】空所の直後には先行詞に付帯する名詞である fame（名声）が置かれ、それが説明されていることから、関係代名詞の所有格 whose が正解となる。

構造 The new recruits ⓢ (finally) had ⓥ a chance ⓞ 〈to meet CEO Jaden Dominguez, 〈whose fame as a business leader they already knew〉〉.

【訳】新入社員たちはついに CEO の Jaden Dominguez 氏と面会する機会を得たが、氏のビジネスリーダーとしての名声に関しては、もうすでに承知していた。

□ recruit　⑧新入社員

36. 正解 (D)

【解説】find という他動詞の直後に、名詞節を作る接続詞の that が省略されていると考えるとよい。that 節の中での主語の部分に空所があるため、主格の代名詞 it が適当。

構造 Black Tower Construction ⓢ was ⓥ pleased ⓒ (to find [it finally won the rights 〈to build the Golden Dragon Amusement Park〉 〈in China〉〉]).

【訳】Black Tower 建設は中国の Golden Dragon 遊園地の建設権をついに獲得したとわかり喜んだ。

□ construction　⑧建設　　□ be pleased to V　⑰V して喜ぶ　　□ right　⑧権利
□ amusement park　⑧遊園地

37. Ms. Akmed picked several team leaders ------- would accompany her on the initial sales meetings in Thailand.
    (A) when
    (B) how
    (C) who
    (D) what

38. Drivers of the P27 Sports Car commonly call ------- the very best vehicle on European roads today.
    (A) them
    (B) their
    (C) it
    (D) its

39. After her meeting, Ms. Sadiche told her colleagues the proposals ------- she made had been warmly received.
    (A) if
    (B) that
    (C) who
    (D) for

40. Quantz Supplies Inc. sells high-end stationery and office appliances, ------- it has steadily increased its quarterly revenue.
    (A) around which
    (B) on top
    (C) down to
    (D) despite

37. 正解 (C)

【解説】先行詞は team leaders という人を表す名詞で、直後には動詞が続いていることから、関係代名詞の主格の who が入ると分かる。

【構造】Ms. Akmed ₍ₛ₎ picked ₍ᵥ₎ several team leaders ₍ₒ₎ ⟨who would accompany her (on the initial sales meetings) ⟨in Thailand⟩⟩.

【訳】Akmed 氏はタイでの最初の販売ミーティングに同伴するチームリーダーたちを数人選出した。

- □ pick 動 選ぶ
- □ accompany 動 同伴する
- □ sales 名 販売

38. 正解 (C)

【解説】call O C は「OをCと呼ぶ」という意味の第5文型の構文。このOの位置には、目的格の代名詞が置かれる。意味の上から、この位置に置かれる代名詞が指す名詞は P27 Sports Car なので、単数の it が正解となる。

【構造】Drivers ₍ₛ₎ ⟨of the P27 Sports Car⟩ (commonly) call ₍ᵥ₎ it ₍ₒ₎ the very best vehicle ₍ᴄ₎ ⟨on European roads today⟩.

【訳】スポーツカー、P27 の運転者は皆、同車を今日のヨーロッパの路上ではまさに最高の乗り物だと呼んでいる。

- □ commonly 副 共通して
- □ vehicle 名 乗物
- □ European 形 ヨーロッパの

39. 正解 (B)

【解説】先行詞 the proposals(提案)で直後には made という他動詞で終わる不完全な文が続いている。このことから関係代名詞の目的格の that が適当。had 以下は述語動詞部分。

【構造】(After her meeting), Ms. Sadiche ₍ₛ₎ told ₍ᵥ₎ her colleagues ₍ₒ₁₎ [₍ₒ₂₎ the proposals ⟨that she made⟩ had been (warmly) received].

【訳】会合の後、Sadiche 氏は同僚に彼女の提案は温かく受け入れられたと告げた。

- □ warmly 副 暖かく

40. 正解 (A)

【解説】空所の後ろが完全な文の形になっているので、前置詞は入らない。around which(〜に基づいて)を入れるのが適当。この around は「〜を中心にして;〜に基づいて」の意味を表す。

【構造】Quantz Supplies Inc. ₍ₛ₎ sells ₍ᵥ₎ high-end stationery and office appliances ₍ₒ₎, ⟨around which it has (steadily) increased its quarterly revenue⟩.

【訳】Quantz Supplies 社は高級文具とオフィス器具を販売しており、それを中心にして四半期ごとの収入を着実に伸ばしている。

- □ on top 熟 上に
- □ down to 熟 〜までさがって
- □ despite 前 〜にもかかわらず
- □ appliance 名 器具
- □ steadily 副 着実に
- □ revenue 名 収入

Lesson 3 適した動詞形の選択
時制と準動詞の判別がポイント

どのような動詞の形が文に適しているかを選ぶ問題でまず重要なのは、それぞれの時制の場合にどのような形が使われるかを知ることです。

現在形
➡動詞の原形

They <u>produce</u> excellent products.
(彼らはすばらしい製品を生産する)

現在形(三人称単数の主語)
➡動詞の原形+s

The company <u>produces</u> excellent products.
(その会社はすばらしい製品を生産する)

現在進行形
➡be動詞+現在分詞形

He <u>is working</u> in that office currently.
(彼は現在その事務所で働いている)

過去進行形
➡be動詞の過去形+現在分詞形

She <u>was working</u> in that office then.
(彼女はその時その事務所で働いていた)

未来形
➡will +動詞の原形

I <u>will visit</u> your office in the afternoon.
(私はあなたの事務所を午後に訪れるつもりです)

現在完了形
➡have +過去分詞形

We <u>have finished</u> the work.
(私たちは仕事をもう終えている)

現在完了形(三人称単数の主語)
➡has +過去分詞形

The company <u>has released</u> a new product.
(その会社は新製品をもう発表した)

現在完了進行形
➡have[has] +been +現在分詞形

The employees <u>have been working</u> for hours.
(従業員は何時間も働いている)

過去完了形
➡had +過去分詞

They <u>had finished</u> the job when I arrived.
(私が到着した時には彼らはもう仕事を終えていた)

同時に、能動態・受動態についても注意しましょう。

受動態　　　　　　　　The company is known for its excellent products.
➡be動詞＋過去分詞　　（その会社はその優秀な製品で知られている）

これら時制に関する理解を試す例題を見てみましょう。

> 例題：The multinational company has recently ------- the increase of the sales at a press conference, where many potential customers gather.
>
> (A) announce　　(B) announcing　　(C) announced　　(D) announces

正解　**(C)**
訳　その多国籍企業は最近、多くの潜在的な顧客が集まる記者会見の場で売り上げの増加を発表した。
【解説】空所の前には、副詞の recently をとばすと、has があるので、これは現在完了形だと考えます。現在完了形は have [has] ＋過去分詞形なので、(C) announced が正解となります。このように、空所の前後からヒントとなるものを見つけ、適切な時制を選択しましょう。

◎主語と述語動詞の対応には特に注意

特に主語と述語動詞が離れている場合には、**主語が単数であるか複数であるかをよく見極めた上で**、動詞を選ぶことが重要です。

◎準動詞の選択

　準動詞とは、動詞の形を変えて様々な別の品詞の働きをさせるもののことを言います。準動詞には、**動名詞、不定詞、分詞、分詞構文**があり、それぞれの形と働きを知ることがこれらを正確に判別するには重要です。

	形	働き
動名詞	Ving	名詞
不定詞	to V	名詞・形容詞・副詞
分詞	Ving / Vpp	形容詞
分詞構文	Ving / Vpp	副詞

例 **Wearing** a tie is a must in our office.
（私たちの会社ではネクタイは必ず締めなければならない）
➡ Vingが主語の名詞の働きをしています。(動名詞)

例 It is not recommended <u>to work</u> overtime at our office.
（私たちの会社では残業して働くことは推奨されていない）
➡ 形式主語のitを受け、to＋動詞の原形が名詞の働きをしています。(不定詞の名詞的用法)

例 Everybody got something <u>to drink</u> during the break.
（休憩時間には皆何か飲むものを買った）
➡ to＋動詞の原形が形容詞の働きをしています。(不定詞の形容詞的用法)

例 I went into the office <u>to talk</u> to my boss.
（私は上司と話すためにオフィスに入った）
➡ to＋動詞の原形が副詞の働きをしています。(不定詞の副詞的用法)

例 Who is that person <u>talking</u> to the boss?
（上司と話しているあの人は誰ですか）
➡ 現在分詞が形容詞の働きをしています。(分詞)

例 Where is the parcel <u>delivered</u> this morning?
(朝、配達されてきた小包はどこですか)
➡過去分詞が形容詞の働きをしています。(分詞)

例 The plane will take off at eight, <u>arriving</u> at its destination at eleven.
(飛行機は8時に離陸し、11時に目的地に到着します)
➡現在分詞が副詞の働きをしています。(分詞構文)

例 <u>Surprised</u> at the news, the CEO called all the directors.
(ニュースに驚いて、CEOはすべての取締役に電話をかけた)
➡過去分詞が副詞の働きをしています。(分詞構文)

これらの準動詞が個別にきちんと理解できていることを前提として、その使い方を知っているかどうかを試すのがこのタイプの問題です。

例題：All the employees working in our office were invited to the party ------- the 100th anniversary of the organization.

(A) celebrated　　(B) celebration　　(C) celebrating　　(D) celebrity

---

正解　(C)

訳　私たちのオフィスで働く全社員が、会社の100周年を祝うパーティーに招待された。

【解説】派生語の理解と合わせて、分詞の力を試す問題となっています。空所以下は、partyという名詞を修飾する形容詞的な働きをしているので、ここではその働きをする現在分詞か過去分詞が答えになると考えることができます。「パーティー」は「100周年を祝う」側なわけですから、能動的な意味を持つ現在分詞の(C)celebratingが答えとなるわけです。ちなみに(B)celebrationは「祝福」、(D)celebrityは「有名人」という名詞です。

EXERCISES

空所補充：各文を完全な形にするために、必要な語句を1つだけ選んでください。

1. A factory in Bratislava ------- textiles had 25% more output than its counterpart in Cracow.
   - (A) producing
   - (B) produced
   - (C) produces
   - (D) will be producing

2. Team Leader Luis Pradesh ------- the new invoicing procedures to his colleagues before the shipment of goods was dispatched.
   - (A) will explain
   - (B) explaining
   - (C) explains
   - (D) had explained

3. Mont Joli Resort offers luxurious accommodations and a wide range of winter sports, such as -------, almost year-round.
   - (A) skied
   - (B) skiing
   - (C) will ski
   - (D) been skied

4. CEO Roger Marquez asked the board members ------- both the advantages and disadvantages of the proposed merger before voting.
   - (A) will be considering
   - (B) considered
   - (C) to consider
   - (D) are considering

全部で40問あります。1問20秒、13分20秒での完答を目指して挑戦しましょう。
すべて解答してから＜正解と解説＞と照合してください。

1. 正解　(A)
【解説】述語動詞はhadだと考えられるので、textilesまでが主語になるようにする。which producesの意味を表す現在分詞producingを空所に入れれば正しい形になる。

構造　A factory〈in Bratislava〉〈producing textiles〉had 25% more output (than its counterpart〈in Cracow〉).

【訳】織物を製造するブラチスラヴァの工場の生産高は、クラクフの同種の工場よりも25％多かった。

□ textile　　名 織物　　　　　　　□ output　　名 生産高　　　　　　□ counterpart　名 互いによく似たもの

2. 正解　(D)
【解説】before（～する前に）の意味から考えて、「説明した」のは商品の発送よりも前のことである。そこで、商品が発送された時点で既に完了していた事実を表す過去完了形（had explained）を使う。

構造　Team Leader Luis Pradesh had explained the new invoicing procedures (to his colleagues) (before the shipment〈of goods〉was dispatched).

【訳】チームリーダーのLuis Pradesh氏は、商品を発送する前に同僚たちに送り状を作る手順を説明していた。

□ invoice　　動 送り状を作成する　　□ procedure　名 手順　　　　　　□ shipment　名 発送
□ goods　　　名 商品；積荷　　　　　□ dispatch　　動 発送する

3. 正解　(B)
【解説】such as ～は「たとえば～のような」という意味で、前置詞に準ずる働きをする。後ろには名詞または動名詞が来るので、skiing（スキーをすること）を入れるのが正しい。

構造　Mont Joli Resort offers luxurious accommodations and a wide range of winter sports,〈such as skiing〉, (almost year-round).

【訳】Mont Joli Resortは、豪華な宿泊設備とスキーなど幅広いウインタースポーツをほぼ1年中提供する。

□ luxurious　　形 豪華な　　　　　　□ accommodations　名 宿泊設備　　□ range　名 幅；範囲
□ A such as B　熟 BのようなA　　　　□ year-round　副 一年中

4. 正解　(C)
【解説】ask ～ to Vで「～にVするよう頼む」の意味を表すので、空所にはto considerが入る。ask＋that節は「～ということを要求する」の意味になるが、that節中の動詞は（demandなどの場合と同様に）原形でなければならない。

構造　CEO Roger Marquez asked the board members to consider both the advantages and disadvantages〈of the proposed merger〉(before voting).

【訳】CEOのRoger Marquez氏は、投票の前に合併計画案の利点と欠点の両方を考慮するよう理事たちに依頼した。

□ board member　名 重役　　　　　　□ advantage　名 有利　　　　　　□ disadvantage　名 不利
□ proposed　　　形 提案された　　　　□ vote　動 投票する

適した動詞の選択　61

5. Staff ------- to work through their lunches can buy meals from any of the vending carts in the front lobby to take to their desks.
   (A) preferring
   (B) will prefer
   (C) prefer
   (D) been preferred

6. Mr. Chagaev was out of the office ------- with clients in the morning, but returned later to do some paperwork.
   (A) has conferred
   (B) conferring
   (C) will be conferred
   (D) will confer

7. Many consumers find ------- goods from large discount chains preferable to other options such as neighborhood shops.
   (A) been purchased
   (B) purchasing
   (C) have purchased
   (D) will have purchased

8. Reports suggest recruiters ------- it difficult to fill vacancies in the engineering sector because fewer students choose the subject.
   (A) will be finding
   (B) are found
   (C) have been found
   (D) to find

5. 正解 (A)

【解説】can buy が述語動詞だと考えられるので、who prefer の意味を表す現在分詞 preferring を空所に入れる。文全体の述語動詞 can buy があるため、(C) prefer は使えない。

構造 Staff ⓢ ⟨preferring to work (through their lunches)⟩ can buy ⓥ meals ⓞ (from any ⟨of the vending carts ⟨in the front lobby⟩⟩) (to take to their desks).

【訳】昼食時間にも仕事をしたいスタッフは、フロントのロビーにある販売ワゴンのどれかで食事を買い、自分の机に持ち込むことができる。

☐ meal ⓝ 食事　　　　　　　☐ vend ⓥ 売る

6. 正解 (B)

【解説】空所の前までが完全な文の形になっているので、空所には述語動詞の形は入らない。「〜しながら」の意味を表す分詞構文 (conferring) を使えば正しい形の文ができる。

構造 Mr. Chagaev ⓢ was ⓥ1 (out of the office) (conferring (with clients) (in the morning)), but returned ⓥ2 (later) (to do some paperwork).

【訳】Chagaev 氏は午前中オフィスを出て依頼主と面談したが、書類の整理をするために後で戻った。

☐ confer with 〜 熟 〜と協議する　　☐ client ⓝ 依頼人　　　☐ paperwork ⓝ 文書事務

7. 正解 (B)

【解説】find O C (O が C だとわかる) の C として preferable (好ましい) を使う形を考え、空所には動名詞の purchasing (購入すること) を入れる。これ以外の選択肢を find の後ろに置くのは、明らかに不自然な形である。

構造 Many consumers ⓢ find ⓥ [ⓞ purchasing goods (from large discount chains)] preferable ⓒ (to other options ⟨such as neighborhood shops⟩).

【訳】多くの消費者は、大きな安売りチェーンから商品を買う方が近所の店など他の手段よりも好ましいと考えている。

☐ purchase ⓥ 購入する　　　☐ option ⓝ 選択　　　　☐ neighborhood ⓝ 近所の

8. 正解 (A)

【解説】文の構造から考えて空所には述語動詞が入るが、空所の後ろに目的語の it があるので、find を受動態 (be found) の形で入れることはできない。未来の一時的状態 (〜していることになるだろう) を表す未来進行形の will be finding を入れるのが正しい。

構造 Reports ⓢ suggest ⓥ [ⓞ recruiters will be finding it difficult [to fill vacancies ⟨in the engineering sector⟩ (because fewer students choose the subject)]].

【訳】報告が示唆するところでは、工学科を選択する学生の減少により、求人担当者は工学部門の求人を満たすのは難しいことになると見ている。

☐ suggest ⓥ 示唆する　　　　☐ recruiter ⓝ 求人担当者　　☐ fill in 熟 埋める
☐ vacancy ⓝ 欠員　　　　　　☐ engineering ⓝ 工学

9. Senior executives ------- Ms. Dominguez's report for one month by the time any feedback on it is given.
   (A) will have been evaluating
   (B) evaluated
   (C) to evaluate
   (D) had been evaluated   Ⓐ Ⓑ Ⓒ Ⓓ

10. Nowadays, executives from the operations department regularly ------- the Vietnam facility to check on output.
   (A) will visit
   (B) visiting
   (C) visit
   (D) been visited   Ⓐ Ⓑ Ⓒ Ⓓ

11. Shoppers at Reco-Mart are now able ------- products out before they buy them as part of a special promotion.
   (A) to test
   (B) tested
   (C) will test
   (D) testing   Ⓐ Ⓑ Ⓒ Ⓓ

12. The Office Supreme Desk Chair is designed to make ------- in front of computer terminals for long periods as comfortable as possible.
   (A) being sitting
   (B) sitting
   (C) sat
   (D) will have been sitting   Ⓐ Ⓑ Ⓒ Ⓓ

9. 正解 (A)

【解説】by the time以下は、現在時制で未来の内容を表している。そこで空所には、「～するまでに1カ月間ずっと評価し続けていることになるだろう」（意見が出される未来の時点まで継続する動作）の意味を表す未来完了進行形を入れる。evaluateは「評価する」の意味。

構造 Senior executives (S) will have been evaluating (V) Ms. Dominguez's report (O) (for one month) (by the time any feedback ⟨on it⟩ is given).

【訳】上級管理職たちは、どんな意見が出されるにせよDominguez氏の報告書を評価するのに1カ月かかるだろう。

- by the time S V 熟 SがVするまでに

10. 正解 (C)

【解説】nowadays（このごろ）は現在形とともに使う副詞。recently（最近）は過去形または現在完了形とともに使うことも、合わせて覚えておくこと。

構造 (Nowadays), executives (S) ⟨from the operations department⟩ (regularly) visit (V) the Vietnam facility (O) (to check on output).

【訳】このごろは、業務部の幹部たちが生産高を点検するためにベトナムの施設を定期的に訪問している。

- executive 名 幹部
- operations department 名 業務部

11. 正解 (A)

【解説】be able to Vで「Vすることができる」の意味になるので、空所にはto testを入れる。test outは「～を実地に試す」の意味。

構造 Shoppers (S) ⟨at Reco-Mart⟩ are (V) (now) able (C) to test products out (before they buy them) (as part of a special promotion).

【訳】Reco-Martの買い物客は、特別キャンペーンの一環として、今なら買う前に製品を実際に使ってみることができる。

- promotion 名 販売促進

12. 正解 (B)

【解説】makeの後ろには目的語が必要。make O C（OをCにする）の形を利用して、Oの位置に動名詞（sitting）を使って「長時間コンピューターの端末の前に座ること」という形を作れば正しい文になる。

構造 The Office Supreme Desk Chair (S) is designed (V) (to make [sitting (in front of computer terminals) (for long periods)] as comfortable as possible).

【訳】Office Supreme Desk Chairは、長時間にわたってコンピューター端末の前に座るのをできるだけ楽にするよう設計されている。

- terminal 名 端末
- comfortable 形 快適な

13. Vice-president Ahmed ------- the acquisition of a competitor for over three weeks by Monday.
    (A) negotiates
    (B) will have been negotiating
    (C) has been negotiated
    (D) will negotiate

    Ⓐ Ⓑ Ⓒ Ⓓ

14. As part of its mission to make shopping easier for parents, shoe store AJ & Co. ------- special equipment for measuring children's feet.
    (A) to carry
    (B) carries
    (C) been carried
    (D) will have been carried

    Ⓐ Ⓑ Ⓒ Ⓓ

15. Evening security guards must switch off all air conditioning units and lights ------- energy.
    (A) to conserve
    (B) will be conserving
    (C) has been conserved
    (D) conserves

    Ⓐ Ⓑ Ⓒ Ⓓ

16. Ryker and Miyazawa Consulting seeks ------- financial support for its customers under the best possible terms.
    (A) been secured
    (B) secured
    (C) to secure
    (D) be secured

    Ⓐ Ⓑ Ⓒ Ⓓ

13. 正解 (B)

【解説】未来のある時点（次の月曜日）までずっと継続している動作（「3週間以上ずっと交渉し続けているだろう」）を表すには、未来完了進行形を使う。

構造 Vice-president Ahmed ⓢ will have been negotiating ⓥ the acquisition ⓞ 〈of a competitor〉 (for over three weeks) (by Monday).

【訳】Ahmed副社長は、月曜日にはライバル社の買収交渉を始めてから3週間以上になるだろう。

☐ negotiates 働交渉する　　☐ acquisition 名買収　　☐ competitor 名競争相手

14. 正解 (B)

【解説】カンマの前は修飾語句なので、空所に述語動詞を入れないと文が成り立たない。carry は「(店が品物を)扱っている」の意味だから、受動態(will have been carried)だと意味をなさない。

構造 (As part 〈of its mission〉〈to make shopping easier (for parents)〉), shoe store AJ & Co. ⓢ carries ⓥ special equipment ⓞ 〈for [measuring children's feet]〉.

【訳】御父母の皆様にとっての買い物の利便性を高める策の一部として、AJ & Co.靴店はお子様の足のサイズを測る特殊装置をご用意しています。

☐ mission 名任務　　☐ equipment 名機器；備品；設備　　☐ measure 働測る
☐ feet 名foot（足）の複数形

15. 正解 (A)

【解説】空所の前までが完全な文の形になっているので、空所以下は修飾語句の働きをする。目的を表す不定詞を使って「エネルギーを節約するために (to conserve energy)」という形を作れば、正しい文になる。

構造 Evening security guards ⓢ must switch off ⓥ all air conditioning units and lights ⓞ (to conserve energy).

【訳】夜間担当の警備員はエネルギー節約のために、すべてのエアコンと電灯のスイッチを切らねばならない。

☐ security guard 名警備員　　☐ air conditioning unit 名エアコン

16. 正解 (C)

【解説】secure は形容詞として使われた場合には、「安全な」という意味になる。seek to V (V するよう努める) の形を利用して secure を動詞として使うのが正しい。

構造 Ryker and Miyazawa Consulting ⓢ seeks ⓥ [ⓞ to secure financial support 〈for its customers〉 (under the best possible terms)].

【訳】Ryker and Miyazawa Consultingは、可能な限り最高の条件で顧客に財政支援を保証しようとしている。

☐ secure 働保証する　　☐ support 名援助　　☐ terms 名条件

適した動詞の選択

17. The New York Tire Co. encourages its workers ------- a healthy lifestyle through using its company gym.
   (A) will adopt
   (B) has adopted
   (C) adopting
   (D) to adopt

18. At his performance review last May, Mr. Jafargholi's supervisor ------- him on his excellent problem-solving abilities.
   (A) will congratulate
   (B) been congratulated
   (C) is congratulating
   (D) congratulated

19. Statistics state that over 48% of employees ------- to use carpools eventually do so.
   (A) will have urged
   (B) have urged
   (C) urging
   (D) urged

20. Holders of the Platinum Plus Business Credit Card ------- to interest-free credit for the first 90 days of the account.
   (A) entitles
   (B) has been entitled
   (C) will be entitled
   (D) are entitling

17. 正解 (D)

【解説】encourage 〜 to V で「〜に V するよう勧める；奨励する」の意味を表す。encourage の後ろに that 節を置く形は誤り。adopt は「採用する」の意味。

構造 The New York Tire Co.(S) encourages(V) its workers(O) to adopt a healthy lifestyle(C) (through [using its company gym]).

【訳】New York Tire 社は、会社のジムの利用を通じて健康的なライフスタイルを採るよう社員に奨励している。

☐ healthy　 形 健康な　　　　　　☐ gym　 名 ジム

18. 正解 (D)

【解説】last は「この前の」の意味。last May は過去のことだから、時制は過去形にする。

構造 (At his performance review last May), Mr. Jafargholi's supervisor(S) congratulated(V) him(O) (on his excellent problem-solving abilities).

【訳】5月の勤務評定で、Jafargholi 氏の上司は彼の優れた問題解決能力をほめたたえた。

☐ performance review　 名 勤務評定　　　☐ congratulate A on B　 熟 A に B のことで祝賀する
☐ ability　 名 能力　　　　　　　　　　☐ excellent　 形 非常に優れた

19. 正解 (D)

【解説】空所に述語動詞を入れると do so の働きが説明できないので、that 節中の主語は over 〜 carpools の部分だと考える。urge 〜 to V (V するよう〜に促す) の形を利用して空所に過去分詞の urged を入れれば、「〜するよう促された社員たち」という正しい意味になる。

構造 Statistics(S) state(V) [(O) that over 48% ⟨of employees ⟨urged to use carpools⟩⟩ (eventually) do so].

【訳】統計が示すところでは、カープールを利用するよう促された社員の48%以上が最終的にそれを実行している。

☐ statistics　 名 統計　　　　　　☐ employee　 名 社員　　　　　　☐ carpool　 名 輪番相乗り
☐ eventually　 副 結局は

20. 正解 (C)

【解説】entitle は「〜に資格を与える」という意味の他動詞で、be entitled to ＋名詞で「〜の資格がある」の意味を表す。be entitled to V (V する資格がある) という形でも使う。この問いでは、現在完了形は意味的に不自然。

構造 Holders(S) ⟨of the Platinum Plus Business Credit Card⟩ will be entitled(V) (to interest-free credit) (for the first 90 days ⟨of the account⟩).

【訳】Platinum Plus Business クレジットカードの所有者は、最初の90日間は無利子で支払い猶予が認められる。

☐ holder　 名 所有者　　　　　　☐ interest-free　 形 無利子の　　　　☐ credit　 名 支払い猶予期間
☐ account　 名 信用取引

適した動詞の選択

21. Instead of simply -------, corporate entrants at the Asia-International IT Award seek to showcase their best products and services.
- (A) wins
- (B) has won
- (C) will win
- (D) winning

22. In this week's edition of EuroBusiness magazine, Professor John Hoffman ------- the impact of economic regulations on importers.
- (A) has been discussed
- (B) will be discussed
- (C) discusses
- (D) discussing

23. Hi Miss Magazine editions ------- online are cheaper to subscribe to and receive daily updates.
- (A) will upload
- (B) uploaded
- (C) are uploading
- (D) have been uploading

24. Data entry mistakes are common in -------, and cannot be avoided entirely even by the most experienced clerks.
- (A) accounting
- (B) account
- (C) accounted
- (D) being accounted

21. 正解 (D)

【解説】instead of ～は「～の代わりに；～しないで」という意味の前置詞の働きをするので、後ろに動詞を置くときは動名詞（winning）にする。

構造 (Instead of simply winning), [corporate entrants]ₛ ⟨at the Asia-International IT Award⟩ seek_v [to showcase their best products and services]_o.

【訳】単に勝てばよいというのではなく、Asia-International IT Awardへの参加企業は最高の製品とサービスを見せようと務める。

- □ simply 副単に；簡単に
- □ entrant 名参加者
- □ showcase 動見せる

22. 正解 (C)

【解説】主語が人間だから、受動態（be discussed）にするのは不自然。discussing だけでは述語動詞になれないので、現在形の discusses を選ぶ。

構造 (In [this week's edition] ⟨of EuroBusiness magazine⟩), Professor John Hoffmanₛ discusses_v [the impact]_o ⟨of economic regulations⟩ ⟨on importers⟩.

【訳】EuroBusiness誌の今週号で、John Hoffman教授は経済規制が輸入業者に与える影響を論じている。

- □ edition 名版
- □ economic 形経済の
- □ regulation 名規制
- □ importer 名輸入業者

23. 正解 (B)

【解説】upload は「～をアップロードする」という意味の他動詞で、空所の後ろに目的語がないから will upload のような形では入れられない。are を述語動詞と考え、空所に過去分詞の uploaded を入れて「アップロードされた版」とすれば意味が通じる。

構造 [Hi Miss Magazine editions]ₛ ⟨uploaded online⟩ are_v cheaper_c (to subscribe to and receive_v daily updates_o).

【訳】インターネットにアップロードされたHi Miss Magazineの版は、購読が安上がりで、毎日更新を受けられる。

- □ subscribe to ～ 熟～を(予約)購読する
- □ update 名最新情報

24. 正解 (A)

【解説】account（口座；説明）と accounting（会計；経理）との意味の違いに注意。ここでは文脈から考えて accounting が入る。

構造 [Data entry mistakes]ₛ are_v1 common_c (in accounting), and cannot be avoided_v2 (entirely) (even by the most experienced clerks).

【訳】データの入力ミスは経理でよく見られ、最も熟達した事務員でさえ完全に避けることはできない。

- □ accounting 名経理
- □ account 名口座
- □ accounted account の過去分詞形
- □ entry 名入力
- □ common 形よく起こる
- □ avoid 動避ける
- □ entirely 副全く
- □ experienced 形経験を積んだ
- □ clerk 名事務員

25. The distribution managers are obliged ------- drivers to return to the warehouses if weather conditions make roads unsafe.
 (A) ordered
 (B) to order
 (C) will be ordering
 (D) will have been ordered

 Ⓐ Ⓑ Ⓒ Ⓓ

26. If you are interested in ------- information about special offers and events, please check the box at the bottom of the screen.
 (A) received
 (B) receiving
 (C) receives
 (D) to receive

 Ⓐ Ⓑ Ⓒ Ⓓ

27. Customers seeking ------- for an extra 5% discount at Loxis Department Store must register for membership cards before May 10.
 (A) qualified
 (B) qualifies
 (C) qualifying
 (D) to qualify

 Ⓐ Ⓑ Ⓒ Ⓓ

28. The public relations spokeswoman ------- the company's management reorganization later in the afternoon.
 (A) confirm
 (B) has been confirmed
 (C) will be confirming
 (D) to confirm

 Ⓐ Ⓑ Ⓒ Ⓓ

25. 正解 (B)

【解説】oblige 〜 to V で「〜にVすることを強制する」の意味。これを受動態にしたbe obliged to V（〜する義務がある；〜しなければならない）という形を使えば、意味の通る文が完成する。

構造 The distribution managers ⓢ are obliged ⓥ to order drivers to return (to the warehouses) (if weather conditions make roads unsafe).

【訳】流通管理者は、天候により道路が危険になった場合は倉庫へ引き返すよう運転手に指令を出さねばならない。

☐ distribution ㊃流通；配送　　☐ unsafe ㊄危険な

26. 正解 (B)

【解説】inは前置詞だから、後ろに動詞を置くときは動名詞(Ving)にする。interested in receiving で「受け取ることに興味を持つ」の意味になる。

構造 (If you are interested (in [receiving information about special offers and events])), (please) check ⓥ the box ⓞ (at the bottom ⟨of the screen⟩).

【訳】特別奉仕品やイベントに関する情報をご希望の場合は、画面の一番下のチェックボックスをオンにしてください。

☐ offer ㊃提供　　☐ check ㊐印をつける　　☐ screen ㊃画面

27. 正解 (D)

【解説】空所の前のseekを「探し求める」の意味と考えると空所には名詞を入れる必要があるが、選択肢には名詞がないので、seek to V（Vしようと試みる）の形を利用する。qualify for 〜は「〜の資格を得る」の意味。

構造 Customers ⓢ ⟨seeking [to qualify (for an extra 5% discount at Loxis Department Store)]⟩ must register ⓥ (for membership cards) (before May 10).

【訳】Loxis Department Storeで5％の追加割引の資格を希望する顧客は、5月10日よりも前に会員カードに登録しなければならない。

☐ register ㊐登録する　　☐ membership card ㊃会員カード

28. 正解 (C)

【解説】later（後で）とあるので、未来の内容を表す文だとわかる。現在形が確定した予定を表す場合もあるが、それだと空所に入る動詞はconfirmsでなければならないので、確定的な未来の予定を表す未来進行形(will be confirming)を選ぶ。

構造 The public relations spokeswoman ⓢ will be confirming ⓥ the company's management reorganization ⓞ (later) (in the afternoon).

【訳】広報担当者は、午後になってから会社の経営陣の再編を正式に発表する予定だ。

☐ public relations ㊃広報活動　　☐ spokeswoman ㊃広報担当者　　☐ confirm ㊐正式に発表する
☐ reorganization ㊃再編成

29. The CEO met with his personal assistant before ------- the keynote speech at this year's biotech conference.
  (A) been delivered
  (B) delivering
  (C) will have been delivered
  (D) delivers

Ⓐ Ⓑ Ⓒ Ⓓ

30. Milktop Cereals ------- quite well, even though they lack the sugary flavor of other brands.
  (A) have been selling
  (B) be sold
  (C) selling
  (D) to sell

Ⓐ Ⓑ Ⓒ Ⓓ

31. After the seminar ------- on the financial state of the company, audience members will be invited to ask questions.
  (A) is presenting
  (B) presents
  (C) has been presented
  (D) is being presented

Ⓐ Ⓑ Ⓒ Ⓓ

32. All new recruits ------- the three-month probationary period will become eligible for full company benefits.
  (A) will complete
  (B) completing
  (C) completed
  (D) been completed

Ⓐ Ⓑ Ⓒ Ⓓ

29. 正解 (B)

【解説】beforeは接続詞としても前置詞としても使うが、接続詞の場合には後ろにSVの形が必要。前置詞の場合はbefore＋Vingで「Vする前に」の意味を表すので、空所にはdeliveringが入る。deliverは「(演説などを)する」の意味。

構造 The CEO (S) met (V) (with his personal assistant) (before **delivering** the keynote speech (at this year's biotech conference)).

【訳】CEOは、今年の生物工学会議で基調演説を行う前に秘書と面会した。

☐ personal assistant　⑧秘書　　☐ keynote speech　⑧基調演説　　☐ biotech　⑧生物工学
☐ conference　⑧会議

30. 正解 (A)

【解説】カンマの後ろは修飾語句なので、カンマの前の部分が完成した文の形でなければならない。空所には述語動詞が入ることになるので、現在完了進行形(have been selling)が入る。sell wellが「よく売れる」という受動の意味を含む点に注意。

構造 Milktop Cereals (S) **have been selling** (V) (quite well), (even though they lack the sugary flavor 〈of other brands〉).

【訳】Milktop Cerealsは、他の銘柄にあるような甘い味に欠けているが、かなりよく売れ続けている。

☐ even though　㉘たとえ…..でも　　☐ lack　⑩欠く　　☐ sugary　㊗甘い

31. 正解 (C)

【解説】本来はwill have been presentedという未来完了形(の受動態)を使って「開かれ(てしまっ)た後で」の意味を表すべきところを、現在完了形で代用した形。afterは時を表す副詞節を作るので、その節中ではwillは使えない。presentは「公開する」の意味。

構造 (After the seminar **has been presented** (on the financial state 〈of the company〉)), audience members (S) will be invited (V) to ask questions.

【訳】会社の財務状況に関するセミナーが開かれた後、聞き手たちは質問するよう促されるだろう。

☐ state　⑧状況　　☐ audience　⑧聴衆　　☐ invite ～ to V　㊗～にVするように勧める

32. 正解 (B)

【解説】述語動詞はwill becomeだと考えられるので、空所には前の名詞句All new recruits (新入社員全員) を修飾する語句を入れる必要がある。ここではwho completeの意味を表す現在分詞のcompletingを入れるのが正しい。

構造 All new recruits (S), 〈**completing** the three-month probationary period〉 will become (V) eligible (C) (for full company benefits).

【訳】3カ月の研修期間を修了した新入社員は全員、会社の給付を正式に受け取る資格を有することになる。

☐ probationary　㊗見習い中の　　☐ eligible　㊗資格のある　　☐ benefit　⑧給付

33. The marketing division ------- new techniques to measure customer satisfaction with the company's products.
(A) will be produced
(B) to produce
(C) been producing
(D) was producing

34. The enclosed documents ------- your rights and responsibilities as the account owner should be read in full.
(A) details
(B) were detailed
(C) detailed
(D) detailing

35. Projects in the initial stages of ------- are carefully monitored by the CEO, CFO and board of directors.
(A) development
(B) developed
(C) to develop
(D) will develop

36. National officials ------- with financial policies regularly have conferences with bank and investment company presidents.
(A) concerned
(B) concerning
(C) will concern
(D) are concerning

33. 正解 (D)

【解説】形の上から、空所には述語動詞が入る。空所の後ろに目的語に相当する名詞new techniques（新技術）があるので、be produced（生み出される）という受動の形は入れられない。したがって過去進行形のwas producingが正解。

構造 The marketing division (s) was producing (v) new techniques (o) ⟨to measure customer satisfaction ⟨with the company's products⟩⟩.

【訳】マーケティング部門は、自社製品に対する顧客の満足度を測定する新技術を生み出しつつあった。

- □ marketing 名マーケティング；市場調査
- □ satisfaction 名満足

34. 正解 (D)

【解説】述語動詞はshould be readの部分と考えられるので、その前が全部主語となるよう、which detailの意味を表す現在分詞detailingを空所に入れる。detailは「詳しく述べる」の意味。

構造 The enclosed documents (s) ⟨detailing your rights and responsibilities ⟨as the account owner⟩⟩ should be read (in full).

【訳】アカウント所有者としてのご自身の権利と責任を詳述した同封書類を、隅々までお読みください。

- □ enclosed 形同封の
- □ document 名書類
- □ responsibility 名責任
- □ account 名アカウント

35. 正解 (A)

【解説】ofは前置詞だから、後ろに動詞を置くときはその目的語の名詞の働きをする語が入るので、development（発展；展開）が正解。

構造 Projects (s) ⟨in the initial stages ⟨of development⟩⟩ are (carefully) monitored (v) (by the CEO, CFO and board of directors).

【訳】展開の初期段階にある事業は、CEO、CFOおよび重役会によって注意深く監視される。

- □ stage 名段階
- □ carefully 副注意深く
- □ monitor 動監視する
- □ board of directors 名重役会

36. 正解 (A)

【解説】concernedは「関連している」という意味の形容詞で、ここでは直前のnational officialsという名詞句を後ろから修飾している。concerned with ～で「～と関連している」という意味になる。concerning ～も「～に関しての」という意味だがwithは必要ない。

構造 National officials (s) ⟨concerned with financial policies⟩ (regularly) have (v) conferences (o) (with bank and investment company presidents).

【訳】金融政策に携わる国家公務員たちは、銀行および投資会社のトップと定期的に会議を開く。

- □ national official 名国家公務員
- □ investment 名投資

適した動詞の選択 77

37. Employee schedules at Juson Home & Garden are flexible enough to help staff ------- their work and home lives.
   (A) will balance
   (B) balancing
   (C) has balanced
   (D) balance

   Ⓐ Ⓑ Ⓒ Ⓓ

38. All media has been completely ------- in the digital age.
   (A) revolution
   (B) revolutionize
   (C) will revolutionize
   (D) revolutionized

   Ⓐ Ⓑ Ⓒ Ⓓ

39. Ms. Chang explained that ------- individuals by phone to see whether they could use the company's products is the core responsibility of a sales representative.
   (A) contacts
   (B) will contact
   (C) contacting
   (D) been contacted

   Ⓐ Ⓑ Ⓒ Ⓓ

40. As their costs ------- last quarter, some airlines bought fuel at fixed prices to avoid future price rises.
   (A) were fluctuating
   (B) will fluctuate
   (C) fluctuates
   (D) will have been fluctuated

   Ⓐ Ⓑ Ⓒ Ⓓ

37. 正解 (D)

【解説】help ～ (to) V は「～が V するのを助ける」という意味の構文で、to を使わずに原形になることがあるので注意。balance はここでは「バランスをとる」という意味の動詞として用いられている。

構造 Employee schedules ⓢ ⟨at Juson Home & Garden⟩ are ⓥ flexible enough ⓒ (to help staff balance their work and home lives).

【訳】Juson Home & Garden の社員の勤務スケジュールは、社員が仕事と家庭とのバランスをとりやすいよう融通がきく。

☐ flexible 圏融通のきく

38. 正解 (D)

【解説】revolutionize は「大変革する」という意味で、主に他動詞として用いられる。ここでは直前に be 動詞があることから、現在完了形の受動態と考え、過去分詞を選択すればよい。revolution は「革命」という意味の名詞。

構造 All media ⓢ has been (completely) revolutionized ⓥ (in the digital age).

【訳】すべての伝達媒体はデジタル時代となり、完全に変革された。

☐ media 图伝達媒体　　☐ completely 副完全に

39. 正解 (C)

【解説】that の前に先行詞がないから、that は関係代名詞ではない。そこで that を「～ということ」の意味を表す接続詞と解釈すると、その節の主語として動名詞の contacting (連絡すること) を使えばよいことがわかる。この節の述語動詞は is である。

構造 Ms. Chang ⓢ explained ⓥ [ⓞ that [contacting individuals (by phone) (to see [whether they could use the company's products])] is the core responsibility ⟨of a sales representative⟩].

【訳】客の一人一人に電話で連絡を取り、会社の製品を使えたかどうかを確かめることが営業マンの核心をなす仕事だ、と Chang 氏は説明した。

☐ individual 图個人　　☐ core 圏核となる　　☐ responsibility 图責任

40. 正解 (A)

【解説】主節の動詞 bought が過去形なので、その時制に一致させて過去進行形の were fluctuating を空所に入れる。fluctuate は「変動する」の意味。

構造 (As their costs were fluctuating (last quarter)), some airlines ⓢ bought ⓥ fuel ⓞ (at fixed prices) (to avoid future price rises).

【訳】この前の四半期には価格が不安定だったので、一部の航空会社は将来の価格上昇を避けるために固定価格で燃料を購入した。

☐ cost 图価格　　☐ fuel 图燃料　　☐ fixed 圏固定した
☐ rise 图上昇

適した動詞の選択

Lesson 4

意味や用法が適した**形容詞・副詞の選択**
まぎらわしい単語をきっちり区別せよ！

　文の構造や意味を複合的に考えて、最も適した形容詞や副詞を選択する問題です。こうした問題ではまぎらわしい形容詞や副詞が選択肢に並べられ、その意味や用法が理解できているかが試されます。

まぎらわしい形容詞・副詞の例

□ considerable	相当な	□ sensible	分別のある
□ considerate	思いやりのある	□ sensitive	敏感な
□ respectable	立派な；まともな	□ successful	成功した
□ respectful	敬意に満ちた	□ successive	連続する
□ respective	それぞれの		
		□ priceless	非常に貴重な
		（= invaluable）	
□ industrial	工業の	□ valueless	価値がない
□ industrious	勤勉な	□ valuable	価値がある

□ late	形 副	遅い；遅く
□ later	副 形 後で；後の／ 形 副 lateの比較級
□ latest	形 最新の／ 形 副 lateの最上級
□ lately	副 最近

　このタイプの問題は、これらの区別を知っていて、前後の文の内容がわかれば解けます。普段からこのようなまぎらわしいものをしっかりと区別して覚えておくようにしましょう。

> 例題: The manager told the workers to go back to their ------- cubicle and continue their work after giving them an urgent order.
>
> (A) respect　　(B) respective　　(C) respectful　　(D) respectable

正解　**(B)**

訳　課長は、緊急の指示を与えた後、職員に個々のブースに戻って仕事を続けるように指示した。

【解説】(A)respectは「尊敬する」という意味の動詞なのでこの位置には置けません。(C)respectfulは「敬意に満ちた」、(D)respectableは「立派な；まともな」という意味なので文意に適していません。「それぞれの」という意味の(B)respectiveが正解となるわけです。

　このようなタイプの設問に強くなるには、はっきり言ってしまうと、**語彙力を強化するしかありません**。できるだけ例文を利用しながら、まぎらわしい語の区別になじむことが重要です。

◎形容詞と副詞の区別には特に注意
　形容詞と副詞が選択肢中にあり、文の形からそのどちらを使うのか決定するタイプの問題も重要です。基本的には、**形容詞は名詞を修飾し、副詞は名詞以外のものを修飾**します。また、「名詞＋ly」は形容詞、「形容詞＋ly」は副詞になるというルールも今一度確認しましょう。

◎比較表現にも要注意
　また、-er / -est、more / mostによる比較級・最上級の変化にも留意する必要があります。たとえば、直後に接続詞の**thanがあるような場合には、比較級**の形容詞や副詞が入るわけです。

EXERCISES

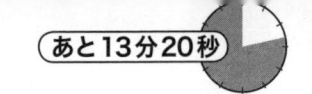

空所補充：各文を完全な形にするために、必要な語句を1つだけ選んでください。

1. Visitors to the Low Valley Boutique have ------- choice in brand, price and style.
   (A) maximal
   (B) maximize
   (C) maximally
   (D) maximization

2. Please place the books on their ------- shelves.
   (A) respectable
   (B) respective
   (C) respecting
   (D) respects

3. Accommodations at the Little Cherry Inn are regarded as ------- spacious, given how small it looks from the outside.
   (A) astonish
   (B) astonishingly
   (C) astonishes
   (D) astonishment

4. As facilities director, Ms. M'tebe is ------- concerned about the rise in the vacancy rate at the Kinshasa Montaga Hotel.
   (A) understanding
   (B) understood
   (C) understandably
   (D) understandable

全部で40問あります。1問20秒、13分20秒での完答を目指して挑戦しましょう。
すべて解答してから＜正解と解説＞と照合してください。

1. 正解 (A)

【解説】choice は have の目的語となる名詞なので、その前には形容詞の maximal（最大限の）を入れると意味が通じる。反対語は minimal（最小限の）。

構造 Visitors ⓢ ⟨to the Low Valley Boutique⟩ have ⓥ maximal choice ⓞ ⟨in brand, price and style⟩.

【訳】Low Valley Boutique への来客は、ブランド、価格、スタイルの点で最大限の選択ができる。

- □ maximize　動最大にする
- □ maximally　副最大限に
- □ maximization　名最大化
- □ choice　名選択；選ばれた物

2. 正解 (B)

【解説】their（所有格）と shelves（名詞）との間に空所があるので、形容詞の respective（それぞれの）を選ぶ。respectable（立派な）、respecting（〜に関して）では意味が通じない。

構造 Please place ⓥ the books ⓞ ⟨on their respective shelves⟩.

【訳】本はそれぞれの棚に置いてください。

- □ respectable　形立派な
- □ respecting　前〜に関して
- □ respects　動尊敬する
- □ place　動置く
- □ shelves　名 shelf（棚）の複数形

3. 正解 (B)

【解説】regarded as spacious で「広々としているとみなされる」という意味が完結するので、空所には spacious を修飾する副詞の astonishingly（驚くほど）を入れる。

構造 Accommodations ⓢ ⟨at the Little Cherry Inn⟩ are regarded ⓥ ⟨as astonishingly spacious⟩, (given [how small it looks ⟨from the outside⟩]).

【訳】Little Cherry Inn の宿泊設備は、外側からはいかに小さく見えるかを考えると、驚くほどゆったりしていると考えられる。

- □ astonish　動驚かす
- □ astonishment　名驚き
- □ inn　名ホテル
- □ spacious　形広々とした
- □ given　前……であることを考慮に入れると

4. 正解 (C)

【解説】空所に何も入れなくても文が成り立つので、副詞の understandably（理解できることだが；当然のことではあるが）を入れる。

構造 ⟨As facilities director⟩, Ms. M'tebe ⓢ is ⓥ (understandably) concerned ⓒ ⟨about the rise ⟨in the vacancy rate⟩ ⟨at the Kinshasa Montaga Hotel⟩⟩.

【訳】施設部長として、M'tebe 氏が Kinshasa Montage Hotel の空室率の上昇を心配しているのは当然だ。

- □ understanding　名理解
- □ understood　形了解済みの
- □ understandable　形理解できる
- □ be concerned about 〜　熟〜について心配している
- □ vacancy　名空室

意味や用法が適した形容詞・副詞の選択

5. Stocks reacted ------- to new information about the economy, rising 3% in morning trading.
(A) positives
(B) positively
(C) positive
(D) positivism

6. The breakdown of the assembly line ------- shut the Cairo factory for two days while repairs were made.
(A) effective
(B) effects
(C) effected
(D) effectively

7. The CubeVox MP3 player is the ------- of the three new models by Mogo Electronics, with a trendy design and bright colors.
(A) popularly
(B) popular
(C) most popular
(D) more popular

8. The annual shareholders meeting is ------- held on the weekends so that even small investors can attend.
(A) deliberate
(B) deliberation
(C) deliberately
(D) deliberates

5. 正解 (B)
【解説】react は自動詞。reacted to ～で「～に反応した」の意味になるので、空所には reacted を修飾する副詞の positively（積極的に）を入れる。

構造 Stocks ⓢ reacted ⓥ (positively) (to new information ⟨about the economy⟩), (rising 3% (in morning trading)).

【訳】株は新しい経済情報に積極的に反応して、午前中の取引で3％上がった。

- □ positives 名陽性
- □ positive 形明確な
- □ positivism 名積極性
- □ stocks 名株

6. 正解 (D)
【解説】空所に何も入れなくても文が成り立つので、空所には動詞の shut を修飾する副詞の effectively（事実上）を入れる。

構造 The breakdown ⓢ ⟨of the assembly line⟩ (effectively) shut ⓥ the Cairo factory ⓞ (for two days) (while repairs were made).

【訳】組み立てラインの故障により、Cairo工場は修理中の2日間事実上閉鎖された。

- □ effective 形効力のある
- □ effects 名結果
- □ effected effect の過去（分詞）形
- □ breakdown 名故障
- □ shut 動閉鎖する

7. 正解 (C)
【解説】空所の後ろが「3つの新モデルのうちで」の意味なので、最上級の形容詞 the most popular を入れると意味が通じる。the は空所の後ろに省略された player につくと考える。

構造 The CubeVox MP3 player ⓢ is ⓥ the most popular ⓒ (of the three new models ⟨by Mogo Electronics⟩), (with a trendy design and bright colors).

【訳】CubeVox MP3 プレーヤーは、流行のデザインと明るい色で、Mogo Electronics の3つの新モデルのうち最も人気がある。

- □ popularly 副一般に；広く
- □ popular 形人気のある
- □ trendy 形最新流行の

8. 正解 (C)
【解説】is held（行われる）だけで意味が通じるので、空所には修飾語の働きをする副詞の deliberately（熟慮して；意図的に）を入れる。

構造 The annual shareholders meeting ⓢ is (deliberately) held ⓥ (on the weekends) (so that even small investors can attend).

【訳】年次株主総会は、小口投資家でも出席できるよう配慮して週末に行われる。

- □ deliberate 形慎重な 動熟考する
- □ deliberation 名熟考
- □ deliberates 動熟考する
- □ annual shareholders meeting 名年次株主総会
- □ so that S can V 熟 SがVできるように
- □ investor 名投資家

意味や用法が適した形容詞・副詞の選択

9. The Cool Breeze air conditioner was put through ------- quality checks before being approved for sale in stores.
- (A) extending
- (B) extends
- (C) extensively
- (D) extensive

Ⓐ Ⓑ Ⓒ Ⓓ

10. The sale of the fish processing factory near Oslo came after months of ------- speculation about it in the business press.
- (A) intensely
- (B) intensify
- (C) intense
- (D) intensity

Ⓐ Ⓑ Ⓒ Ⓓ

11. Analysts ------- predict a rise in the number of people purchasing consumer durables such as washing machines.
- (A) confidence
- (B) confidently
- (C) confident
- (D) confiding

Ⓐ Ⓑ Ⓒ Ⓓ

12. Best Home Co. spokesman Jayesh Mattell ------- confirmed that the company will make no cuts in its workforce.
- (A) directions
- (B) directed
- (C) directive
- (D) directly

Ⓐ Ⓑ Ⓒ Ⓓ

9. 正解 (D)

【解説】quality checks（品質検査）という名詞句を修飾する部分なので、形容詞のextensive（包括的な；徹底的な）を選ぶ。-iveは主に形容詞を作る接尾辞。

構造 The Cool Breeze air conditioner ⓢ was put ⓥ (through extensive quality checks) (before [being approved (for sale in stores)]).

【訳】Cool Breezeエアコンは、店頭販売を認可される前に厳しい品質検査を受けた。

- □ extending　extendの現在分詞形
- □ extends　動広げる
- □ extensively　副広範囲に
- □ put A through B　熟AをBに通して調べる
- □ approve　動認可する

10. 正解 (C)

【解説】speculation（憶測）という名詞を修飾する部分なので、形容詞のintense（激しい；盛んな）が入る。itはthe saleを受ける代名詞。

構造 The sale ⓢ ⟨of the fish processing factory ⟨near Oslo⟩⟩ came ⓥ (after months of intense speculation ⟨about it⟩ ⟨in the business press⟩).

【訳】オスロ近くの魚の加工場は、経済ジャーナリズムで何カ月も盛んに憶測された末に売却された。

- □ intensely　副激しく
- □ intensify　動強める
- □ intensity　名激しいこと
- □ process　動加工する

11. 正解 (B)

【解説】主語と動詞の間に空所があるので、動詞のpredictを修飾する副詞のconfidently（確信して）を選ぶ。「自信に満ちたアナリストたち」ならconfident analystsの語順になる。

構造 Analysts ⓢ (confidently) predict ⓥ a rise ⓞ ⟨in the number ⟨of people ⟨purchasing consumer durables ⟨such as washing machines⟩⟩⟩⟩.

【訳】アナリストたちは、洗濯機のような耐久消費財を購入する人々の数が増えると自信を持って予言している。

- □ confidence　名信頼
- □ confident　形確信している
- □ confiding　形人を信じやすい
- □ predict　動予言する
- □ consumer durables　名耐久消費財

12. 正解 (D)

【解説】主語と動詞の間に空所があるので、動詞のconfirmed（確認した）を修飾する副詞のdirectly（直接に）を入れる。

構造 Best Home Co. spokesman Jayesh Mattell ⓢ (directly) confirmed ⓥ [ⓞ that the company will make no cuts ⟨in its workforce⟩].

【訳】Best Home社の広報担当Jayesh Mattellは、会社が人員削減を一切行わないことを直接確認した。

- □ directions　名指導
- □ directed　形指揮された
- □ directive　形指示の
- □ spokesman　名広報担当者
- □ make cuts in ～　熟～を削減する
- □ workforce　名労働力

意味や用法が適した形容詞・副詞の選択

13. LiteGuard provides ------- skin protection against harsh sun rays, whether out at the beach or in your own backyard.
(A) except
(B) exceptionally
(C) excepting
(D) exceptional

Ⓐ Ⓑ Ⓒ Ⓓ

14. Yu Corporation is ------- unknown outside of South Korea, but is steadily increasing its overseas sales.
(A) relativity
(B) relatively
(C) relates
(D) relative

Ⓐ Ⓑ Ⓒ Ⓓ

15. All patient records in the clinic are classified as confidential because of their ------- nature.
(A) sensitive
(B) sensitively
(C) sensitivity
(D) sensible

Ⓐ Ⓑ Ⓒ Ⓓ

16. While speaking to customers, it is important to maintain a ------- tone of voice at all times.
(A) professional
(B) profession
(C) professionally
(D) professions

Ⓐ Ⓑ Ⓒ Ⓓ

13. 正解 (D)

【解説】skin protection（肌の保護）という名詞を修飾する部分なので、形容詞の exceptional（例外的な；特に優れた）を選ぶ。

構造 LiteGuard ⓢ provides ⓥ exceptional skin protection ⓞ 〈against harsh sun rays〉, (whether (out at the beach) or (in your own backyard)).

【訳】LiteGuardは、屋外の浜辺にいても自宅の裏庭にいても、強い日光から肌を守る優れた効果を提供する。

- □ except 動除く
- □ exceptionally 副例外的に
- □ excepting 前〜を除いて
- □ harsh 形厳しい
- □ sun rays 名日光
- □ backyard 名裏庭

14. 正解 (B)

【解説】is unknown で「知られていない」という意味になるので、空所には修飾語として働く副詞の relatively（比較的）を入れる。unknown が前の名詞を修飾すると解釈すれば空所には名詞も入りうるが、relativity（関連性）や relative（親戚）では意味が通じない。

構造 Yu Corporation ⓢ is ⓥ1 (relatively) unknown ⓒ (outside of South Korea), but is (steadily) increasing ⓥ2 its overseas sales ⓞ.

【訳】Yu社は韓国以外には比較的知られていないが、海外での売り上げを着実に伸ばしている。

- □ relativity 名関連性
- □ relates 動関係づける
- □ relative 名親類 形関係のある

15. 正解 (A)

【解説】nature（性質）という名詞を修飾する部分なので、形容詞の sensitive（敏感な；デリケートな；機密扱いの）を選ぶ。

構造 All patient records ⓢ 〈in the clinic〉 are classified ⓥ (as confidential) (because of their sensitive nature).

【訳】その医院のすべての患者のカルテは、要注意の性格を持つため部外秘に分類されている。

- □ sensitively 副繊細に
- □ sensitivity 名感じやすさ
- □ sensible 形分別のある
- □ patient 名患者
- □ clinic 名診療所
- □ classify A as B 熟AをBに分類する
- □ confidential 形秘密の

16. 正解 (A)

【解説】a と名詞 tone の間に空所があるので、tone を修飾する形容詞の professional（プロの；専門家の）を入れるのが適当。

構造 (While speaking to customers), it ⓢ is ⓥ important ⓒ [to maintain a professional tone 〈of voice〉 (at all times)].

【訳】客と話している間は、常にプロの口調を維持することが重要である。

- □ profession 名職業
- □ professionally 副職業的に
- □ tone of voice 熟口調

17. The board of directors acted ------- fast to increase the amount of investments in its India facilities.
    (A) surprises
    (B) surprise
    (C) surprisingly
    (D) surprising

    Ⓐ Ⓑ Ⓒ Ⓓ

18. As business development head, Mr. Assad has to remain ------- not only among potential clients but in the general community as well.
    (A) visibility
    (B) visible
    (C) vision
    (D) visions

    Ⓐ Ⓑ Ⓒ Ⓓ

19. Many of the older ------- buildings near the port have been demolished and replaced with new office towers.
    (A) industrializing
    (B) industrial
    (C) industrialize
    (D) industrious

    Ⓐ Ⓑ Ⓒ Ⓓ

20. Greco Construction Co. stays ------- with all European safety rules regarding its worksites.
    (A) complies
    (B) complying
    (C) compliance
    (D) compliant

    Ⓐ Ⓑ Ⓒ Ⓓ

17. 正解　(C)

【解説】act（行動する）は自動詞だから、後ろに名詞は置けない。副詞のfastを修飾する副詞 surprisingly（驚くほど）を入れて「驚くべき速さで」とすれば意味が通じる。

構造　The board of directors ⓢ acted ⓥ (surprisingly fast) (to increase the amount of investments ⟨in its India facilities⟩).

【訳】役員会はインドの施設への投資額を増やすために驚くべき速さで行動した。

☐ surprise　⑩驚かす　⑧驚き　　☐ surprising　⑱驚くべき　　☐ the amount of ～　⑨～の総額

18. 正解　(B)

【解説】remain C は「C のままである」の意味で、後ろには名詞か形容詞を置く。ここでは「見えるままでいる；顔を出し続ける」とすれば意味が通じるので、形容詞の visible（目に見える）を選ぶ。

構造　(As business development head), Mr. Assad ⓢ has to remain ⓥ visible ⓒ (not only (among potential clients) but (in the general community as well)).

【訳】事業開発の長として、Assad氏は潜在的な顧客だけでなく地域全般にも顔を売り続けねばならない。

☐ visibility　⑧視界　　　　　☐ vision　⑧先見性；幻　　　　☐ development　⑧開発
☐ potential　⑱潜在的な　　　☐ general　⑱全般的な　　　　☐ community　⑧地域

19. 正解　(B)

【解説】buildings という名詞を修飾する部分なので、形容詞の industrial（産業の）が適当。industrious（勤勉な）では意味が通じない。

構造　Many ⓢ ⟨of the older industrial buildings ⟨near the port⟩⟩ have been demolished and replaced ⓥ (with new office towers).

【訳】港の近くの古い産業ビルの多くは、取り壊されて新しいオフィスタワーに建て替えられた。

☐ industrializing　industrializeの現在分詞形　　☐ industrialize　⑩工業化する　　☐ industrious　⑱勤勉な
☐ port　　　⑧港　　　　　　　　　　　　　　　☐ demolish　⑩破壊する
☐ replace A with B　⑨AをBと取り替える

20. 正解　(D)

【解説】stay C で「C のままでいる」を意味するので、C の位置には形容詞の compliant（遵守した）を入れるのが適当。stay は目的語を取る動詞ではないので、名詞の compliance は入れられない。

構造　Greco Construction Co. ⓢ stays ⓥ compliant ⓒ (with all European safety rules ⟨regarding its worksites⟩).

【訳】Greco建設は、建築現場に関する全ヨーロッパの安全規則を遵守し続けている。

☐ complies　⑩従う　　　　　　☐ complying　complyの現在分詞形　　☐ compliance　⑧従うこと
☐ safety rules　⑧安全規則　　☐ regarding　⑪～に関して　　　　　☐ worksite　⑧作業現場

21. The audience listened ------- as the medical experts outlined their views on the pharmaceutical industry.
   (A) attentively
   (B) attention
   (C) attending
   (D) attentiveness

22. The Strawberry Fire motorcycle has ------- become the most popular vehicle of its kind in Australia.
   (A) appearing
   (B) appearance
   (C) apparent
   (D) apparently

23. Rafael Conference Center is the ------- location for holding large-scale conventions in the city of Berne.
   (A) preference
   (B) prefers
   (C) preferably
   (D) preferred

24. Ms. Zim said ------- action was needed if the corporation was to regain its position as market leader.
   (A) decide
   (B) decision
   (C) decisive
   (D) deciding

21. 正解 (A)
【解説】asは「……するとき；……しながら」の意味の接続詞。as以下は修飾節だから取り外して考えると、自動詞listenedの後ろに置けるのは副詞のattentively（注意深く）のみ。

構造 The audience ⓢ listened ⓥ (attentively) (as the medical experts outlined their views ⟨on the pharmaceutical industry⟩).

【訳】聴衆は、医療専門家たちが製薬業界に関する意見を概括している間、注意深く耳を傾けた。

- attention ㊔注意
- attending ㊦主治医である
- attentiveness ㊔注意深さ
- medical ㊦医療の
- expert ㊔専門家
- outline ㊓概説する
- view ㊔意見
- pharmaceutical ㊦製薬の
- industry ㊔業界

22. 正解 (D)
【解説】hasを「持っている」の意味と解釈して空所に名詞を入れると、後ろのbecomeとつながらない。has becomeを現在完了形と考えて、空所には修飾語として働く副詞のapparently（見たところ（〜らしい））を入れる。

構造 The Strawberry Fire motorcycle ⓢ has (apparently) become ⓥ the most popular vehicle ⓒ ⟨of its kind⟩ (in Australia).

【訳】Strawberry Fireのオートバイは、オーストラリアの同種の乗り物の中で最も人気があるようだ。

- appearing appearの現在分詞形
- appearance ㊔出現
- apparent ㊦明白な

23. 正解 (D)
【解説】theと名詞location（場所）の間に空所があるので、形容詞のpreferred（好ましい）を選ぶ。

構造 Rafael Conference Center ⓢ is ⓥ the preferred location ⓒ ⟨for [holding large-scale conventions]⟩ ⟨in the city of Berne⟩.

【訳】Rafael Conference Centerは、ベルン市で大規模な会議を開くのに好ましい場所である。

- preference ㊔優先
- prefers ㊓好む
- preferably ㊓できれば
- large-scale ㊦大規模な
- convention ㊔会議

24. 正解 (C)
【解説】saidに続くthat節中の主語はactionだから、それを修飾する形容詞のdecisive（決定的な；断固とした）を選ぶ。動詞decide（決心する）の後ろに名詞を置くときはonが必要だから、deciding actionとは言えない。

構造 Ms. Zim ⓢ said ⓥ [ⓞ decisive action was needed (if the corporation was to regain its position ⟨as market leader⟩)].

【訳】Zim氏は、会社が市場のリーダーとしての地位を取り戻すつもりなら決然とした行動が必要だと言った。

- decision ㊔決定
- deciding decideの現在分詞形
- regain ㊓取り戻す

意味や用法が適した形容詞・副詞の選択

25. Mr. Allen presented his analysis of the situation to the management team in a highly ------- manner.
   (A) persuasion
   (B) persuades
   (C) persuasive
   (D) persuasively

26. Staff are ------- forbidden to use their cell phones during work hours, except for personal emergencies.
   (A) expression
   (B) expressly
   (C) expresses
   (D) expressive

27. Residents of the apartment building have access to ------- underground parking spaces that can accommodate up to 250 vehicles.
   (A) securitize
   (B) securing
   (C) securely
   (D) secure

28. There will be only ------- room for ships while structural reinforcements are made at the harbor.
   (A) limiting
   (B) limited
   (C) limitation
   (D) limits

25. 正解 (C)

【解説】manner という名詞を修飾する部分なので、形容詞の persuasive (説得力のある) を選ぶ。前に副詞 (highly) があるので、名詞の persuasion を入れることはできない。

構造 Mr. Allen ₍ₛ₎ presented ₍ᵥ₎ his analysis ₍ₒ₎ ⟨of the situation⟩ (to the management team) (in a highly persuasive manner).

【訳】Allen 氏は非常に説得力のある方法で経営陣に状況分析を提示した。

- ☐ persuasion 名説得
- ☐ persuades 動説得する
- ☐ persuasively 副説得力をもって
- ☐ analysis 名分析
- ☐ situation 名状況
- ☐ highly 副非常に
- ☐ manner 名方法

26. 正解 (B)

【解説】are forbidden (禁じられている) だけで意味が通じるので、空所には副詞の expressly (はっきりと) が入る。

構造 Staff ₍ₛ₎ are (expressly) forbidden ₍ᵥ₎ to use their cell phones (during work hours), (except for personal emergencies).

【訳】スタッフは個人的な急用の場合以外は勤務時間中に携帯電話を使うことを明確に禁じられている。

- ☐ expression 名表現
- ☐ expresses 動表現する
- ☐ expressive 形表現の
- ☐ except for 〜 熟〜を除いては
- ☐ emergency 名緊急事態

27. 正解 (D)

【解説】underground parking spaces (地下駐車場) という名詞句を修飾する部分なので、形容詞の secure (安全な) を選ぶ。securing だと「地下駐車場を守ること」となり意味が通じない。

構造 Residents ₍ₛ₎ ⟨of the apartment building⟩ have ₍ᵥ₎ access ₍ₒ₎ ⟨to secure underground parking spaces⟩ ⟨that can accommodate up to 250 vehicles⟩⟩.

【訳】そのアパートの居住者は、250 台まで車を収容する安全な地下駐車場を利用できる。

- ☐ securitize 動証券化する
- ☐ securing secure の現在分詞形
- ☐ securely 副安全に
- ☐ resident 名居住者
- ☐ have access to 〜 熟〜を利用できる
- ☐ accommodate 動収容する
- ☐ up to 〜 熟 (最高) 〜まで

28. 正解 (B)

【解説】room (余地；スペース) を修飾する形容詞の limited (限られた) を入れるのが適当。limiting (制限する；極端な) では意味が通じない。

構造 There will be ₍ᵥ₎ only limited room ₍ₛ₎ ⟨for ships⟩ (while structural reinforcements are made (at the harbor)).

【訳】港で施設の補強工事が行われているので、船舶の入港には限られたスペースしかなくなるだろう。

- ☐ limiting 動制限する
- ☐ limitation 名制限
- ☐ limits 名限度
- ☐ structural 形構造の
- ☐ harbor 名港

29. Telephone representatives are encouraged to use their time as ------- as possible, and are offered rewards for reaching sales targets.
(A) production
(B) productive
(C) productively
(D) producing

30. Loden Corporation negotiated a ------- better price for its goods after going into business with a local distributor.
(A) considerably
(B) consider
(C) considerable
(D) considering

31. Ms. Pizarro was ------- twice as fast as her colleagues at summarizing reports for her supervisors.
(A) practical
(B) practicality
(C) practically
(D) practices

32. Large homes are becoming ------- expensive for first-time buyers, though smaller ones continue to sell well.
(A) prohibitively
(B) prohibit
(C) prohibits
(D) prohibiting

29. 正解 (C)

【解説】as ... as possible（できるだけ…）の空所には、形容詞または副詞が入る。ここでは as possible がなくても文が成り立つので、副詞の productively（生産的に）を選ぶ。

構造 Telephone representatives ⓢ are encouraged ᵥ₁ to use their time (as productively as possible), and are offered ᵥ₂ rewards (for [reaching sales targets]).

【訳】電話営業の担当者は時間をできるだけ生産的に使うよう奨励され、売り上げ目標に到達すれば報酬を与えられる。

- □ production　名生産
- □ productive　形生産的な
- □ producing　produce の現在分詞形
- □ representative　名セールスマン；担当者
- □ reward　名報酬
- □ sales targets　名販売目標

30. 正解 (A)

【解説】形容詞の better を修飾する副詞の considerably（かなり；相当に）を選ぶ。

構造 Loden Corporation ⓢ negotiated ᵥ a considerably better price ⓞ ⟨for its goods⟩ (after [going into business (with a local distributor)]).

【訳】Loden 社は、地元の販売店と取引を始めた後で商品価格をかなり下げる取り決めをした。

- □ consider　動よく考える
- □ considerable　形かなりの
- □ considering　前〜を考えると
- □ negotiate　動取り決める
- □ go into business　熟取引を始める
- □ distributor　名販売店

31. 正解 (C)

【解説】主語が人間だから、practicality（実用性）を be 動詞の補語として使うのは意味的に不自然。主語が単数だから、practices も形の上で使えない。修飾語として働く副詞の practically（実質上；ほとんど）を入れると意味が通じる。

構造 Ms. Pizarro ⓢ was ᵥ (practically) twice as fast ⓒ (as her colleagues) (at summarizing reports (for her supervisors)).

【訳】Pizarro 氏は、上司への報告を要約するスピードにかけては同僚たちのほぼ2倍だった。

- □ practical　形現実的な
- □ practicality　名実用性
- □ practices　名慣習
- □ summarize　動要約する

32. 正解 (A)

【解説】become expensive で「高価になる」という自然な意味になるので、空所には becoming を修飾する副詞の prohibitively（阻止するに十分→（値段が）法外に）を入れる。

構造 Large homes ⓢ are becoming ᵥ (prohibitively) expensive ⓒ (for first-time buyers), (though smaller ones continue to sell well).

【訳】小さな家はよく売れ続けているが、大きな家は初めて家を買う人にとっては法外に高価な値段になりつつある。

- □ prohibit　動禁止する
- □ prohibiting　prohibit の現在分詞形
- □ first-time　形初めての
- □ buyer　名購入者
- □ continue to V　熟Vし続ける

意味や用法が適した形容詞・副詞の選択

33. Mr. Heo spoke ------- to the assembled reporters about Sung Group's decision to begin exporting to Europe.
    (A) enthusiasm
    (B) enthusiastic
    (C) enthusiastically
    (D) enthuses

34. The computer network system which is adopted in this company is quite ------- compared with those used in other old companies.
    (A) progressive
    (B) progress
    (C) progression
    (D) progressively

35. Upgrades were applied ------- to all computers throughout Masterson Inc.'s main network.
    (A) systematically
    (B) systems
    (C) systematize
    (D) systematic

36. The ------- market dominance of Wow Now Chocolate Bar is due to its unique blend of chocolate, peanuts and caramel.
    (A) literary
    (B) literate
    (C) literal
    (D) literally

33. 正解 (C)

【解説】spokeの目的語になるのは言語名(Englishなど)だけで、それ以外の場合は自動詞として使う。したがって空所にはspokeを修飾する副詞のenthusiastically(熱心に)が入る。

構造 Mr. Heo (s) spoke (v) (enthusiastically) (to the assembled reporters) (about Sung Group's decision ⟨to begin exporting to Europe⟩).

【訳】Heo氏は、Sungグループがヨーロッパへの輸出を開始するという決定に関して、集められた記者たちに熱心に語った。

- ☐ enthusiasm ⑧熱狂
- ☐ enthusiastic ⑱熱狂的な
- ☐ enthuses ⑩熱狂させる
- ☐ assembled ⑱集められた
- ☐ reporter ⑧報道記者
- ☐ export ⑩輸出する

34. 正解 (A)

【解説】この文の主語はThe computer network systemで述語動詞はis。そのisの補語となっている部分なので、形容詞progressive(進歩的な)が正解。

構造 The computer network system (s) ⟨which is adopted (in this company)⟩ is (v) quite progressive (c) (compared with those ⟨used (in other old companies)⟩).

【訳】この企業で採用されているそのコンピュータネットワークシステムは、他の古い体質の企業と比べ、かなり革新的なものだ。

- ☐ progress ⑧進歩
- ☐ progression ⑧進行
- ☐ progressively ⑩次第に
- ☐ adopt ⑩採用する
- ☐ compared with ~ ⑲~と比べて

35. 正解 (A)

【解説】空所に何も入れなくても文が成り立つので、appliedを修飾する副詞のsystematically(組織的に)を入れる。applied systems(応用されたシステム)は文脈に合わない。

構造 Upgrades (s) were applied (v) (systematically) (to all computers) (throughout Masterson Inc.'s main network).

【訳】Masterson社のメインネットワークを通じて、すべてのコンピュータに一律にアップグレードが適用された。

- ☐ systems ⑧組織
- ☐ systematize ⑩組織化する
- ☐ systematic ⑱組織的な
- ☐ throughout ⑪~を通じて

36. 正解 (C)

【解説】market dominance(市場の支配)を修飾する形容詞として適当なのはliteral(文字通りの)。

構造 The literal market dominance (s) ⟨of Wow Now Chocolate Bar⟩ is (v) due to its unique blend ⟨of chocolate, peanuts and caramel⟩.

【訳】Wow Now Chocolate Barが文字通り市場を支配しているのは、チョコレート、ピーナツ、キャラメルの独特のブレンドによる。

- ☐ literary ⑱文学の
- ☐ literate ⑱読み書きができる
- ☐ literally ⑩文字通りに
- ☐ unique ⑱独特の

37. The Durand Architectural Prize is presented each year to the individual or corporation with the most ------- impressive designs.
- (A) creatively
- (B) creation
- (C) creating
- (D) creates

38. Ms. Marcos sat down and ------- began to work her way through her assignments for the day.
- (A) method
- (B) methods
- (C) methodical
- (D) methodically

39. Mandarin Grove Park is one of the finest places ------- to spend a lovely afternoon among breathtaking views.
- (A) imagination
- (B) imaginable
- (C) imagining
- (D) imagines

40. SushiNow Restaurant provides excellent choices for those looking for ------- alternatives to burgers or pizzas.
- (A) healthily
- (B) healthy
- (C) healthiest
- (D) healthier

37. 正解 (A)

【解説】the most impressive designs（最も印象的なデザイン）だけでも意味が通じるので、空所にはimpressiveを修飾する副詞のcreatively（独創的に）を入れる。

構造 The Durand Architectural Prize ⓢ is presented ⓥ (each year) (to the individual or corporation ⟨with the most creatively impressive designs⟩).

【訳】Durand建築賞は、最も個性的で印象に残るデザインを発表した個人または企業に対して毎年贈られる。

☐ creation　名創造　　　　☐ creating　createの現在分詞形　　☐ creates　動創造する
☐ prize　　名賞；賞品　　☐ present　動贈呈する　　　　　　☐ individual　名個人

38. 正解 (D)

【解説】andはsat down（座った）とbeganを結びつけていると解釈できるので、空所にはbeganを修飾する副詞のmethodically（整然と；几帳面に）を入れる。work one's way through ～は「～を順番に進める」の意味。

構造 Ms. Marcos ⓢ sat down ⓥ₁ and (methodically) began ⓥ₂ [ⓞ to work her way (through her assignments ⟨for the day⟩)].

【訳】Marcos氏は腰を降ろしてその日の割り当て業務を几帳面に順番に進め始めた。

☐ method　名方法　　☐ methodical　形順序だった　　☐ assignment　名割り当てられた仕事

39. 正解 (B)

【解説】空所に何も入れなくても文が成り立つ点に着目して、修飾語として働く形容詞のimaginable（想像できる）を入れる。最上級の後に置くと、「想像できる最も～な」という意味を表すことができる。

構造 Mandarin Grove Park ⓢ is ⓥ one ⓒ ⟨of the finest places imaginable ⟨to spend a lovely afternoon (among breathtaking views)⟩⟩.

【訳】Mandarin Grove公園は、息を飲むような景色の中ですてきな午後を過ごそうとすれば頭に浮かぶ最高の場所の１つである。

☐ imagination　名想像力　　　☐ imagining　imagineの現在分詞形　　☐ imagines　動想像する
☐ finest　　　fineの最上級　　☐ breathtaking　形息を飲むような　　☐ view　名景色

40. 正解 (D)

【解説】空所の後ろにalternativeという名詞があるので形容詞に絞る。healthyの比較級のhealthier（より健康的な）を選べばよい。those looking はpeople (who are) lookingの意味。

構造 SushiNow Restaurant ⓢ provides ⓥ excellent choices ⓒ (for those ⟨looking for healthier alternatives ⟨to burgers or pizzas⟩⟩).

【訳】SushiNowレストランは、ハンバーガーやピザよりも健康的な料理を求める人々に精選された品ぞろえを提供する。

☐ healthily　　副健康に　　　　　　☐ healty　形健康な　　　　☐ healthiest　healthyの最上級
☐ look for ～　熟～を得ようと求める　☐ alternative　名代用品

Lesson 5

意味や用法が適した**名詞の選択**
英語独特の感覚に注意！

　語彙力を試す問題です。このタイプの設問に強くなるためには、**日本語と英語の差に注意しながら、多くの語彙を吸収**していく必要があります。地理的に隔絶された場所で別個に成長を続けた日英両言語は、多くの単語が非対応です。

　たとえば、日本語では単に「客」というところを、英語ではcustomer（商店の顧客）、client（弁護士などへの依頼客）、guest（招待客）、spectator（観客）……などと複数の単語で使い分けるわけです。

注意すべき名詞の区別①「お金」

「料金」や「お金」に関するまぎらわしい単語をまとめておきます。
この使い分けは日本語とは異なるもので、特に注意が必要です。

☐ change	小銭；おつり
☐ cost	費用；原価
☐ currency	通貨
☐ bill	紙幣；請求書
☐ check	小切手；勘定書
☐ fee	医者や弁護士などの専門サービスに対する謝礼；授業料
☐ tuition	授業料
☐ cash	現金
☐ charge	一般の手数料；公共料金；ホテル代など
☐ account	口座
☐ price	商品の値段
☐ fare	運賃
☐ toll	通行料金；通話料金

> 例題：Because David's insurance had just expired, he was obliged to pay the doctor's ------- in full by himself.
> (A) charge　(B) fee　(C) fare　(D) price

正解　**(B)**

訳　デイビッドの保険は切れたばかりだったので、彼は医療費を全額自己負担しなければならなかった。

【解説】医者のように、資格が必要な専門職のサービスを受け、その謝礼として支払う料金は(B)feeです。(A)chargeは一般の公共サービスや手数料に関して使われます。また、(C)fareは乗り物の運賃に関して使われます。(D)priceは物やサービスの「価格」を意味する言葉です。

注意すべき名詞の区別②「客」

「客」という意味を表すまぎらわしい単語をまとめておきます。

- □ customer　商店の顧客
- □ passenger　乗客
- □ visitor　訪問客；見舞客
- □ tourist　観光客
- □ audience　演劇などの顧客・聴衆
- □ client　弁護士などの依頼人
- □ guest　招待客
- □ spectator　見物人；観客

例
The customer is always right.
（お客様は神様だ）
You're my guest today.
（今日はあなたがお客様ですからね）
Rachel seems to have a visitor.
（レイチェルのところには客が来ているようだ）

EXERCISES

空所補充：各文を完全な形にするために、必要な語句を1つだけ選んでください。

1. Forsyth Materials Co. has to undergo a complete ------- of its business statements and reports every year by an outside auditor.
   (A) appointment
   (B) perspective
   (C) detriment
   (D) examination

2. Any ------- between you and Moraez Group is subject to the terms and conditions set forth below.
   (A) retention
   (B) intrusion
   (C) agreement
   (D) rotation

3. Liberty Mall Café offers a delightful ------- of light refreshments, including donuts and beverages.
   (A) nature
   (B) selection
   (C) growth
   (D) projection

4. Trucks carrying the new machinery were delayed at the ------- by customs officials checking their paperwork.
   (A) limit
   (B) divisor
   (C) border
   (D) separation

全部で40問あります。1問20秒、13分20秒での完答を目指して挑戦しましょう。
すべて解答してから＜正解と解説＞と照合してください。

---

1. 正解 (D)

【解説】has to undergo（〜を受けねばならない）との意味的なつながりから考えて、名詞 examination（調査）を入れるのが適切。

構造 Forsyth Materials Co.₍ₛ₎ has to undergo₍ᵥ₎ a complete examination ₍ₒ₎ ⟨of its business statements and reports⟩ (every year) (by an outside auditor).

【訳】Forsyth Materials 社は、外部の監査官による事業報告書の完全な調査を毎年受けねばならない。

- ☐ appointment　名約束
- ☐ perspective　名展望
- ☐ detriment　名損害
- ☐ undergo　動受ける
- ☐ complete　形完全な
- ☐ statement　名報告書
- ☐ auditor　名会計検査官

---

2. 正解 (C)

【解説】「条件(terms and conditions)に制約される」という内容から考えて、主語となる名詞としては agreement（協定；契約）が適当。

構造 Any agreement ₍ₛ₎ ⟨between you and Moraez Group⟩ is₍ᵥ₎ subject ₍c₎ (to the terms and conditions ⟨set forth below⟩).

【訳】貴社と Moraez グループとの間のいかなる契約も、下記に示された条件の制約を受けます。

- ☐ retention　名保有
- ☐ intrusion　名侵入
- ☐ rotation　名回転
- ☐ set forth　熟明記する
- ☐ below　副下記に

---

3. 正解 (B)

【解説】offers（提供する）の対象となるものとしては、selection が適当。この selection は「選択の対象となる一群の商品；品ぞろえ」の意味を表す。

構造 Liberty Mall Café ₍ₛ₎ offers₍ᵥ₎ a delightful selection ₍ₒ₎ ⟨of light refreshments⟩, ⟨including donuts and beverages⟩.

【訳】Liberty Mall Café は、ドーナツと飲み物を含む魅力的な軽食セットを提供する。

- ☐ nature　名自然
- ☐ growth　名成長
- ☐ projection　名投射
- ☐ delightful　形うれしい
- ☐ refreshments　名軽い飲食物

---

4. 正解 (C)

【解説】customs officials（税関の役人たち）を手がかりにして、空所に border を入れて「国境で(遅れた)」とすれば意味の通る文になる。

構造 Trucks ₍ₛ₎ ⟨carrying the new machinery⟩ were delayed₍ᵥ₎ (at the border) (by customs officials ⟨checking their paperwork⟩).

【訳】新型の機械類を運ぶトラックは、税関職員による書類審査のために国境で遅れた。

- ☐ limit　名限度
- ☐ divisor　名除数
- ☐ separation　名分離
- ☐ machinery　名機械類
- ☐ delay　動遅らせる
- ☐ official　名職員；当局者
- ☐ paperwork　名事務書類

意味や用法が適した名詞の選択

5. The decision to change the product packaging was made in ------- with Oberhaur Incorporated's marketing group.
　(A) accord
　(B) seal
　(C) display
　(D) skill　　　　　　　　　　　　Ⓐ Ⓑ Ⓒ Ⓓ

6. To promote Jane's Kitchen Co.'s new ------- of cherry cookies, sales assistants offered interested shoppers free samples to try in the store.
　(A) length
　(B) time
　(C) point
　(D) line　　　　　　　　　　　　Ⓐ Ⓑ Ⓒ Ⓓ

7. Ms. Yip liked working downtown, but found the ------- to and from her home in the suburbs tiring.
　(A) extension
　(B) accommodation
　(C) permission
　(D) commute　　　　　　　　　Ⓐ Ⓑ Ⓒ Ⓓ

8. Ms. Summers felt the professional ------- between herself and her assistant was based on trust and mutual respect.
　(A) insertion
　(B) causation
　(C) bond
　(D) priority　　　　　　　　　　Ⓐ Ⓑ Ⓒ Ⓓ

5. 正解　(A)

【解説】前後の前置詞とのつながりから、空所に名詞accord（一致）を入れてin accord with ～（～と一致して；～に応じて）という形にすれば意味の通る文になる。

構造 The decision ⓢ ⟨to change the product packaging⟩ was made ⓥ (in accord with Oberhaur Incorporated's marketing group).

【訳】製品のパッケージを変更するという決定が、Oberhaur社の販売促進部の意向に応じて行われた。

- □ seal　　　名印
- □ packaging　名包装箱のデザイン
- □ display　　名陳列
- □ skill　　名熟練

6. 正解　(D)

【解説】名詞lineには「その種のもの；品ぞろえ」の意味があり、new line of ～で「～の新製品」の意味になる。

構造 (To promote Jane's Kitchen Co.'s new line ⟨of cherry cookies⟩), sales assistants ⓢ offered ⓥ interested shoppers ⓞ₁ free samples ⓞ₂ ⟨to try⟩ (in the store).

【訳】Jane's Kitchen社の新製品のチェリークッキーを売り込むために、販売員たちは関心を持った買い物客に店頭で無料の試供品を配った。

- □ length　　名長さ
- □ promote　動宣伝販売する
- □ time　　名時間
- □ interested　形興味を持った
- □ point　　名先端
- □ free sample　名試供品

7. 正解　(D)

【解説】空所の後ろのto and from her home（自宅への、そして自宅からの）との意味的なつながりから、commute（通勤）を選ぶ。

構造 Ms. Yip ⓢ liked ⓥ₁ [ⓞ working downtown], but found ⓥ₂ the commute ⓞ ⟨to and from her home ⟨in the suburbs⟩⟩ tiring ⓒ.

【訳】Yip氏は中心街で働くのが好きだったが、郊外の自宅からの通勤は骨の折れるものだった。

- □ extension　名拡張
- □ downtown　動中心街で[へ]
- □ accommodation　名便宜
- □ suburbs　名郊外
- □ permission　名許可
- □ tiring　形骨の折れる

8. 正解　(C)

【解説】「自分自身と部下との間の～」という文脈から、空所にはbond（絆）を入れるのが適当。後半の「信頼とお互いへの敬意に基づく」という述部とも意味的にうまくつながる。

構造 Ms. Summers ⓢ felt ⓥ [ⓞ the professional bond ⟨between herself and her assistant⟩ was based (on trust and mutual respect)].

【訳】Summers氏は、自分と部下との職務上の絆は信頼とお互いへの敬意に基づいていると感じた。

- □ insertion　名挿入
- □ professional　形職業上の
- □ mutual　形相互の
- □ causation　名原因
- □ be based on ～　熟～に基づいている
- □ respect　名敬意
- □ priority　名優先
- □ trust　名信頼

意味や用法が適した名詞の選択

9. Carlsson Industries reduced its previous ------- on coal and oil by using solar panels at some of its facilities.
 (A) power
 (B) reliance
 (C) interest
 (D) strength

 Ⓐ Ⓑ Ⓒ Ⓓ

10. Observers say smaller businesses must find unique ------- to compete against large companies with lower operating margins.
 (A) resentments
 (B) passages
 (C) assurances
 (D) techniques

 Ⓐ Ⓑ Ⓒ Ⓓ

11. Although online banking is popular, most people still like to have the -------- to visit their branch in person.
 (A) freedom
 (B) arrival
 (C) deliverance
 (D) level

 Ⓐ Ⓑ Ⓒ Ⓓ

12. The GetItClean dishwasher has enough ------- to comfortably hold 27 plates, 12 cups and 10 utensils on its racks.
 (A) capacity
 (B) understanding
 (C) friction
 (D) frequency

 Ⓐ Ⓑ Ⓒ Ⓓ

9. 正解 (B)

【解説】空所の後ろのonに着目してreliance on ~（~への依存）とすれば、reduced（減らした）と意味的にうまくつながる。動詞のrelyは、rely on ~（~に依存する）の形で使う。

【構造】Carlsson Industries ⓢ reduced ⓥ its previous reliance ⓞ 〈on coal and oil〉(by [using solar panels (at some of its facilities)]).

【訳】Carlsson Industriesは、施設の一部で太陽熱パネルを使うことによって、従来の石炭と石油への依存度を減らした。

- □ power ㊤力
- □ previous ㊟以前の
- □ interest ㊤関心
- □ coal ㊤石炭
- □ strength ㊤力
- □ solar panel ㊤太陽電池板

10. 正解 (D)

【解説】「小企業は独自の~を見つけねばならない」という文脈から、空所にはtechniques（技術）を入れるのが適当。

【構造】Observers ⓢ say ⓥ [ⓞ smaller businesses must find unique techniques 〈to compete (against large companies) 〈with lower operating margins〉〉].

【訳】小企業がより低い営業利益率を持つ大企業と競争するためには、独自の技術を開発せねばならないと評者たちは言う。

- □ resentments ㊤憤り
- □ observer ㊤評論家
- □ margin ㊤利ざや
- □ passages ㊤通路
- □ compete against ~ ㊥~と競争する
- □ assurances ㊤保証
- □ operating ㊟営業の

11. 正解 (A)

【解説】「訪問する~を持つ」という文脈から、空所にはfreedom（自由）を入れるのが適当。

【構造】(Although online banking is popular), most people ⓢ (still) like ⓥ [ⓞ to have the freedom 〈to visit their branch (in person)〉].

【訳】オンラインの銀行取引は人気があるが、ほとんどの人々は自ら銀行の支店を訪ねる自由を今でも持ちたがっている。

- □ arrival ㊤到着
- □ branch ㊤支店
- □ deliverance ㊤救出
- □ in person ㊥自ら
- □ level ㊤水準

12. 正解 (A)

【解説】「皿洗い機（dishwasher）は十分な~を持つ」という文脈から、空所にはcapacity（容量）を入れるのが適当。racksとは「皿洗い機内部の仕切り棚」のこと。

【構造】The GetItClean dishwasher ⓢ has ⓥ enough capacity ⓞ 〈to (comfortably) hold 27 plates, 12 cups and 10 utensils (on its racks)〉.

【訳】GetItClean皿洗い機は27点の皿、12点のカップ、10点の器具が棚に楽に収まる十分な容量を持つ。

- □ understanding ㊤理解
- □ comfortably ㊡楽に
- □ friction ㊤摩擦
- □ hold ㊥収容できる
- □ frequency ㊤頻度
- □ utensil ㊤器具

意味や用法が適した名詞の選択

13. Kidsco Toys keeps a cash ------- of €10 billion on hand so that it can fund most of its investments without the need to borrow.
    (A) convenience
    (B) request
    (C) reserve
    (D) attendance

14. Mr. Salvensen's proposal for the business expansion was greeted with ------- by most of the directors.
    (A) enthusiasm
    (B) enclosure
    (C) momentum
    (D) compatibility

15. Passengers can purchase subway ------- from vending machines on the concourse as well as the main office.
    (A) sales
    (B) tokens
    (C) openings
    (D) rails

16. Visitors are required to sign in at the front desk and wait for company staff to serve as their ------- while on the premises.
    (A) agenda
    (B) travel
    (C) escort
    (D) contention

13. 正解 (C)

【解説】「現金の〜を保持している」という文脈から、空所にはreserve（準備金）を入れるのが適当。名詞のreserveは「蓄え；留保」などの意味を表す。

構造 Kidsco Toys(s) keeps(v) a cash reserve(o) 〈of €10 billion〉(on hand) (so that it can fund most 〈of its investments〉〈without the need 〈to borrow〉〉).

【訳】Kidsco Toysは100億ユーロの現金資金が手元にあるので、投資の大半に借り入れ不要で資金を投じることができる。

- ☐ convenience 名便利
- ☐ on hand 熟手元に
- ☐ request 名依頼
- ☐ fund 動資金を提供する
- ☐ attendance 名出席

14. 正解 (A)

【解説】greeted by 〜（〜によって歓迎される）を修飾する副詞句としては、with enthusiasm（熱心に）が適切。

構造 Mr. Salvensen's proposal(s) 〈for the business expansion〉 was greeted(v) (with enthusiasm) (by most 〈of the directors〉).

【訳】事業拡張のためのSalvensen氏の提案は、大部分の重役たちに熱烈に歓迎された。

- ☐ enclosure 名包囲
- ☐ expansion 名拡張；発展
- ☐ momentum 名はずみ
- ☐ compatibility 名適合性

15. 正解 (B)

【解説】tokenとは、地下鉄などで切符代わりに使われる代用硬貨(token coin)のこと。これを知らなくても、purchase（購入する）の目的語として適当なものを消去法で考えれば正解に到達できる。

構造 Passengers(s) can purchase(v) subway tokens(o) (from vending machines 〈on the concourse〉 as well as the main office).

【訳】乗客はメインの売り場だけでなくコンコースの自動販売機でも地下鉄のトークンを購入することができる。

- ☐ sales 名売上高
- ☐ vending machine 名自動販売機
- ☐ openings 名就職口
- ☐ concourse 名コンコース
- ☐ rails 名レール

16. 正解 (C)

【解説】serve as their 〜（彼らの〜として務める）という文脈から、空所にはescort（付き添い）を入れるのが適切。theirはvisitorsを受ける代名詞。

構造 Visitors(s) are required(v) to sign in (at the front desk) and wait for company staff to serve (as their escort) (while on the premises).

【訳】訪問者はフロントで署名し、敷地内にいる間は社員が案内役を務めるのを待つよう求められる。

- ☐ agenda 名協議事項
- ☐ require 動要求する
- ☐ travel 名旅行
- ☐ front desk 名フロント
- ☐ contention 名争い
- ☐ wait for 〜 to V 熟〜がVするのを待つ

17. Transport officials announced that a £2.00 ------- will be imposed on all vehicles using the Tinsdale Motorway.
(A) ride
(B) toll
(C) assembly
(D) stock

Ⓐ Ⓑ Ⓒ Ⓓ

18. Paid subscribers to this Web site receive automatic ------- for all contests and prizes it offers.
(A) exchange
(B) production
(C) script
(D) eligibility

Ⓐ Ⓑ Ⓒ Ⓓ

19. Mr. Palos, the office manager, apologized for the ------- that the fax machine was still out of order.
(A) test
(B) fact
(C) portion
(D) establishment

Ⓐ Ⓑ Ⓒ Ⓓ

20. Officials are organizing a three-day-long festival this summer as a special ------ of the city's 300-year history.
(A) breadth
(B) commemoration
(C) installation
(D) symptom

Ⓐ Ⓑ Ⓒ Ⓓ

17. 正解 (B)

【解説】空所の前に「2ポンド(の)」とあるので、toll（使用料；通行料）を入れるのが適切。toll road は有料道路、toll gate は有料道路の料金所の意味。

構造 Transport officials ⓢ announced ⓥ [ⓞ that a £2.00 toll will be imposed on all vehicles 〈using the Tinsdale Motorway〉].

【訳】交通当局者は、Tinsdale Mortorwayを利用するすべての車両に対して2ポンドの通行料を課すと公表した。

- □ ride ㊂乗ること
- □ transport ㊂輸送機関
- □ assembly ㊂集会
- □ announce ㊐告知する
- □ stock ㊂在庫品
- □ impose A on B ㊍BにAを課す

18. 正解 (D)

【解説】空所の後ろのforとの結びつきを考えながら意味の通る名詞を探すと、eligibility（適格）が最も適当。eligibility for ～で「～への適格性；～の資格」の意味を表す。

構造 Paid subscribers ⓢ 〈to this Web site〉 receive ⓥ automatic eligibility ⓞ 〈for all contests and prizes 〈it offers〉〉.

【訳】当ウェブサイトへの有料の加入者は、当サイトが提供するすべてのコンテンツと賞品の資格を自動的に取得できます。

- □ exchange ㊂交換
- □ subscriber ㊂加入者
- □ production ㊂製品
- □ script ㊂台本

19. 正解 (B)

【解説】「～に対して謝罪する」という文脈と、空所の後ろのthat節の働きから考えて、空所にはfact（事実）が入る。the fact that ～で「～という事実」の意味を表す(that以下は同格節)。

構造 Mr. Palos, the office manager ⓢ, apologized ⓥ (for the fact 〈that the fax machine was (still) out of order〉).

【訳】事務長のPalos氏は、ファクス機がまだ故障中だという事実を謝罪した。

- □ test ㊂検査
- □ apologize for ～ ㊍～のことで謝る
- □ portion ㊂分け前
- □ out of order ㊍故障して
- □ establishment ㊂設立

20. 正解 (B)

【解説】「特別な～として祭りを計画する」という文脈から、空所にはcommemoration（記念）を入れる。

構造 Officials ⓢ are organizing ⓥ a three-day-long festival ⓞ (this summer) (as a special commemoration 〈of the city's 300-year history〉).

【訳】市政300年の歴史の特別記念として、当局者たちは今年の夏に3日間の祭りを計画しているところだ。

- □ breadth ㊂幅
- □ organize ㊐計画する
- □ installation ㊂取付け
- □ symptom ㊂徴候

意味や用法が適した名詞の選択

21. Renters must leave a two-month ------- with the landlord before being allowed to sign a yearlong lease.
    (A) profit
    (B) capital
    (C) deposit
    (D) protection

22. Bygro Inc.'s self-cleaning barbecue grill moved quickly from its ------- as an idea within the technical group to full production and sales.
    (A) motion
    (B) inception
    (C) commerce
    (D) realism

23. DryClean9000.com is an outstanding ------- of a corporation that operates smoothly both on and off line.
    (A) opportunity
    (B) occasion
    (C) strategy
    (D) example

24. B15-TV provides around-the-clock ------- on business and economic news from all over the world.
    (A) commentary
    (B) allowance
    (C) exertion
    (D) subjection

21. 正解 (C)

【解説】「借地人は〜を預けねばならない」という文脈から、空所にはdeposit（手付金；頭金）が入る。depositには銀行預金のほかに「担保；保証金；頭金」の意味がある。

構造 Renters(S) must leave(V) a two-month deposit(O) (with the landlord)(before [being allowed to sign a yearlong lease]).

【訳】借地人は、1年間の借地契約書に署名する許可を得る前に、地主に2か月分の手付金を預けねばならない。

- ☐ profit ㊂利益
- ☐ capital ㊂資本；首都
- ☐ protection ㊂保護
- ☐ renter ㊂借地人
- ☐ leave A with B ㊚AをBに預ける
- ☐ landlord ㊂地主
- ☐ yearlong ㊄1年間続く
- ☐ lease ㊂借地契約

22. 正解 (B)

【解説】moved from A to B（AからBへ移行した）という文構造に着目して、空所にはinception（初め＝beginningの同意語）を入れる。

構造 Bygro Inc.'s self-cleaning barbecue grill(S) moved(V) (quickly)(from its inception ⟨as an idea⟩ ⟨within the technical group⟩)(to full production and sales).

【訳】Bygro社の自洗式バーベキューグリルは、最初の技術班内部の着想の段階から本格生産・販売へと迅速に進んだ。

- ☐ motion ㊂運動
- ☐ commerce ㊂商業
- ☐ realism ㊂現実主義
- ☐ self-cleaning ㊄自己浄化式の
- ☐ move ㊙進展する

23. 正解 (D)

【解説】会社名が主語なので、be動詞の補語としてはexample（例）が適当。「会社＝機会」とか「会社＝戦略」という関係は、意味的に成り立たない。

構造 DryClean9000.com(S) is(V) an outstanding example(C) ⟨of a corporation ⟨that operates (smoothly)(both on and off line)⟩⟩.

【訳】DryClean9000.comは、ネット販売と店頭販売をうまく併用する企業の顕著な例である。

- ☐ opportunity ㊂機会
- ☐ occasion ㊂出来事
- ☐ strategy ㊂戦略
- ☐ smoothly ㊙順調に

24. 正解 (A)

【解説】テレビ放送が提供するものとしては、commentary（時事解説）が適当。commentary on 〜で「〜に関する解説；注釈」の意味を表す。

構造 B15-TV(S) provides(V) around-the-clock commentary(O) ⟨on business and economic news ⟨from all over the world⟩⟩.

【訳】B15-TVは、世界中のビジネスと経済のニュース解説を24時間提供する。

- ☐ allowance ㊂手当
- ☐ exertion ㊂努力
- ☐ subjection ㊂征服
- ☐ around-the-clock ㊄24時間営業の
- ☐ all over the world ㊚世界中

25. Please read the following ------- regarding activities allowed within the stadium before entering.
    (A) possessions
    (B) restrictions
    (C) consistencies
    (D) meetings

26. Vmedia broadband customers are being offered a free ------- to 10Mb, making downloading speeds even quicker.
    (A) dedicator
    (B) position
    (C) conversion
    (D) technology

27. Tennis courts are available to all health club members willing to pay an additional $17 ------- each month.
    (A) force
    (B) fare
    (C) fee
    (D) fine

28. As the candy industry points out, chocolate is high in fat, but is also an important ------- of calcium.
    (A) regard
    (B) number
    (C) period
    (D) source

25. 正解 (B)

【解説】readの目的語として適当なのはrestrictions（制限；規定）。スタジアム入り口に掲示された文面と考えられる。

構造 (Please) read ⓥ the following restrictions ⓞ ⟨regarding activities ⟨allowed (within the stadium)⟩⟩ (before entering).

【訳】ご入場の前に、スタジアム内で許可される活動に関する次の規定をお読みください。

- □ possessions 名財産
- □ consistencies 名堅さ
- □ meetings 名会議
- □ following 形次の
- □ activity 名活動

26. 正解 (C)

【解説】「無料の～が提供される」という文脈に合うのはconversion（変換；切り替え）。convert A to B（AをBに変換する）という動詞の形をもとに考える。

構造 Vmedia broadband customers ⓢ are being offered ⓥ a free conversion ⟨to 10Mb⟩, (making downloading speeds even quicker).

【訳】Vmediaブロードバンドの利用者には10Mbへの無料の切り替えの提供が進んでおり、それによってダウンロードがさらに迅速になる。

- □ dedicator 名献身的な人
- □ position 名位置
- □ technology 名科学技術
- □ free 形無料の

27. 正解 (C)

【解説】似た形の名詞を意味で区別する問題。fee（料金）はクラブなどの入会金、使用料、学費、公共料金、専門職への報酬などの意味で使われる。

構造 Tennis courts ⓢ are ⓥ available ⓒ (to all health club members ⟨willing to pay an additional $17 fee (each month)⟩).

【訳】テニスコートは、月々17ドルの追加料金を進んで支払うすべてのヘルスクラブ会員が利用できる。

- □ force 名力
- □ fare 名運賃
- □ fine 名罰金
- □ be willing to V 熟Vするのをいとわない
- □ additional fee 名追加料金

28. 正解 (D)

【解説】「チョコレートはカルシウム(calcium)の重要な～だ」という文脈に合うのはsource（源）。

構造 (As the candy industry points out), chocolate ⓢ is ⓥ₁ high ⓒ (in fat), but is ⓥ₂ (also) an important source ⓒ ⟨of calcium⟩.

【訳】キャンディー業界が指摘するようにチョコレートには脂肪分が多いが、重要なカルシウム源でもある。

- □ regard 名尊敬
- □ number 名数
- □ period 名期間
- □ point out 熟指摘する
- □ be high in fat 熟脂肪の含量が多い

意味や用法が適した名詞の選択

29. Owners of SWT Electronics appliances can call the customer service helpline to receive expert ------- at any time.
  (A) duration
  (B) advice
  (C) superiority
  (D) schedule   Ⓐ Ⓑ Ⓒ Ⓓ

30. Bahrain is well-known among vacationers looking for sunshine and luxurious --------.
  (A) imaginations
  (B) completions
  (C) referrals
  (D) surroundings   Ⓐ Ⓑ Ⓒ Ⓓ

31. Invoices should be checked over thoroughly to guard against ------- in customer billing.
  (A) unpopularity
  (B) inaccuracies
  (C) insecurities
  (D) dissection   Ⓐ Ⓑ Ⓒ Ⓓ

32. Work ------- are that staff be at their desks by no later than 9:15 A.M., Monday through Saturday.
  (A) connections
  (B) advances
  (C) expectations
  (D) contacts   Ⓐ Ⓑ Ⓒ Ⓓ

29. 正解 (B)

【解説】「専門家の～を受け取る」という文脈に合うのは advice（助言）。helpline は「電話による情報提供サービス」のこと。

構造 Owners ⓢ ⟨of SWT Electronics appliances⟩ can call ⓥ the customer service helpline ⓞ (to receive expert advice) (at any time).

【訳】SWT Electronics 社製の電気製品の持ち主は、専門家の助言を受けるためにいつでも顧客電話サービスに電話をかけることができる。

- ☐ duration ⑧持続
- ☐ superiority ⑧優越
- ☐ schedule ⑧予定
- ☐ appliance ⑧電気器具

30. 正解 (D)

【解説】「行楽客（vacationers）によく知られている」という文脈から、luxurious surroundings（ぜいたくな環境）とすれば意味が通る。

構造 Bahrain ⓢ is ⓥ well-known ⓒ (among vacationers ⟨looking for sunshine and luxurious surroundings⟩).

【訳】バーレーンは陽光とぜいたくな環境を探し求める行楽客の間でよく知られている。

- ☐ imaginations ⑧想像
- ☐ completions ⑧完成
- ☐ referrals ⑧推薦

31. 正解 (B)

【解説】「請求書をチェックする」という前半の文脈から考えて、空所には inaccuracies（誤り）を入れる。もとになる形容詞は accurate（正確な）で、その名詞形 accuracy（正確さ）に否定の接頭辞 in- をつけたもの（不正確さ→誤り）。

構造 Invoices ⓢ should be checked over ⓥ (thoroughly) (to guard against inaccuracies ⟨in customer billing⟩).

【訳】顧客への請求書送付の誤りを防ぐために、請求書は徹底的に隅々までチェックするべきだ。

- ☐ unpopularity ⑧不人気
- ☐ insecurities ⑧不安定なもの
- ☐ dissection ⑧解剖
- ☐ invoice ⑧請求書
- ☐ check over ⓗ調べる
- ☐ thoroughly ⓐ徹底的に
- ☐ guard against ～ ⓗ～を警戒する
- ☐ billing ⑧請求書の送付

32. 正解 (C)

【解説】that は「～ということ」の意味の名詞節を作る接続詞。節中の動詞が be（原形）なので、文全体が要求・提案などのニュアンスを含むと考え、expectations（期待されるもの）を選ぶ。

構造 Work expectations ⓢ are ⓥ [ⓒ that staff be (at their desks) (by no later than 9:15 A.M.), (Monday through Saturday)].

【訳】仕事に期待されるものは、職員は月曜日から土曜日まで午前9時15分までに机についているということである。

- ☐ connections ⑧縁故
- ☐ advances ⑧申し入れ；前進
- ☐ contacts ⑧付き合い
- ☐ no later than ～ ⓗ～よりも遅くなることなく

33. You may get detailed information on your monthly use of city ------- by going to our Web site and entering your account number.
   (A) determinations
   (B) practicalities
   (C) sanctions
   (D) utilities   Ⓐ Ⓑ Ⓒ Ⓓ

34. It is a legal ------- for advisors to warn clients that the value of their stocks may increase or decrease, depending on a number of risk factors.
   (A) obligation
   (B) judge
   (C) survival
   (D) court   Ⓐ Ⓑ Ⓒ Ⓓ

35. Paktor Corporation rewards employees based on their performance rather than their ------- within the firm.
   (A) measure
   (B) attachment
   (C) seniority
   (D) forecast   Ⓐ Ⓑ Ⓒ Ⓓ

36. Mr. Asavi printed out the ------- of the product analyses before faxing them over to the assistant director in Lagos.
   (A) results
   (B) supplies
   (C) greetings
   (D) distances   Ⓐ Ⓑ Ⓒ Ⓓ

33. 正解 (D)
【解説】「市の〜の利用」という文脈に合うのはutilities（公共事業；公共施設；電気・ガス・水道の公共料金）。

構造 You ⓢ may get ⓥ detailed information ⓞ 〈on your monthly use 〈of city utilities〉〉（by [going to our Web site] and [entering your account number]）.

【訳】市の公共料金の月々の使用料の明細は、当ウェブサイトへ行きアカウント番号を入力すれば入手できます。

- ☐ determinations ㊎決定
- ☐ practicalities ㊎実用性
- ☐ sanctions ㊎制裁
- ☐ detailed ㊋詳細な
- ☐ account number ㊎口座番号

34. 正解 (A)
【解説】Itは後ろの不定詞を受ける形式主語。legal（法律上の）の後ろに置く名詞としては、obligation（義務）が適当。

構造 It ⓢ is ⓥ a legal obligation ⓒ (for advisors) [to warn clients [that the value 〈of their stocks〉 may increase or decrease, (depending on a number of risk factors)]].

【訳】いくつかのリスク要因次第で持ち株の価格が上下するかもしれないと、アドバイザーが顧客に警告するのは法的な義務である。

- ☐ judge ㊎審判員
- ☐ survival ㊎生存
- ☐ court ㊎法廷
- ☐ warn ㊐警告する；注意する
- ☐ value ㊎価値
- ☐ decrease ㊐減る
- ☐ depending on 〜 ㊥〜に応じて
- ☐ a number of 〜 ㊥いくらかの〜

35. 正解 (C)
【解説】their performance（彼らの業績）と比較する対象としては、their seniority（彼らの年功）が適切。

構造 Paktor Corporation ⓢ rewards ⓥ employees ⓞ (based on their performance (rather than their seniority 〈within the firm〉)).

【訳】Paktor社は、社内での年功よりもむしろ業績に基づいて社員に報酬を与える。

- ☐ measure ㊎方策
- ☐ attachment ㊎付属品
- ☐ forecast ㊎予報
- ☐ reward ㊐報酬を与える
- ☐ firm ㊎会社

36. 正解 (A)
【解説】print out（印字する；プリントアウトする）の目的語として意味が通るのは、「製品分析の結果(results)」。

構造 Mr. Asavi ⓢ printed out ⓥ the results ⓞ 〈of the product analyses〉 (before faxing them (over) (to the assistant director 〈in Lagos〉)).

【訳】Asavi氏は、製品分析の結果をラゴスの次長にファクスする前に印字した。

- ☐ supplies ㊎必需品
- ☐ greetings ㊎挨拶
- ☐ distances ㊎距離
- ☐ analyses ㊎analysis（分析）の複数形
- ☐ assistant director ㊎次長

37. Job applicants must provide references who can confirm their good character and current work -------.
    (A) reception
    (B) remnants
    (C) status
    (D) adoption   Ⓐ Ⓑ Ⓒ Ⓓ

38. As profits rose, Wonju Clothing Inc. was able to give its machine operators a pay ------- and improved working conditions.
    (A) quality
    (B) raise
    (C) term
    (D) setting   Ⓐ Ⓑ Ⓒ Ⓓ

39. Dentistry 4 US Weekly has the highest ------- in the state among dentists, dental technicians and their patients.
    (A) circulation
    (B) publication
    (C) realization
    (D) notification   Ⓐ Ⓑ Ⓒ Ⓓ

40. Lawyers at Jones & Simpson keep up the ------- of the firm by maintaining a higher than average win percentage for all their cases.
    (A) issue
    (B) memorandum
    (C) contrast
    (D) reputation   Ⓐ Ⓑ Ⓒ Ⓓ

37. 正解 (C)

【解説】referencesは、後ろに関係代名詞のwhoがついていることから、「身元保証人」と解釈する。その人物がconfirm（立証）する対象としては、work status（職務上の地位）が適切。

【構造】Job applicants (S) must provide (V) references (O) 〈who can confirm their good character and current work status〉.

【訳】求職者は、本人の優良な人格と現在の職務上の地位を立証できる身元保証人を用意しなければならない。

- □ reception　名歓迎
- □ job applicant　名求職者
- □ remnants　名残存者
- □ character　名人格
- □ adoption　名採用
- □ current　形今の

38. 正解 (B)

【解説】pay raise（昇給）は重要な連語。単にraise（賃上げ）とも言う。

【構造】(As profits rose), Wonju Clothing Inc. (S) was (V) able (C) to give its machine operators a pay raise and improved working conditions.

【訳】利益が増すにつれて、Wonju Clothing社は機械作業員たちに昇給と労働条件の改善を提供することができた。

- □ quality　名質
- □ machine operator　名機械工
- □ term　名期間
- □ pay　名給料
- □ setting　名背景
- □ improve　動改善する

39. 正解 (A)

【解説】雑誌が「持っている」ものとして適当なのは、circulation（発行部数）。population（人口）などと同様に、circulationの多少はlarge / smallやhigh / lowで表す。

【構造】Dentistry 4 US Weekly (S) has (V) the highest circulation (O) 〈in the state〉〈among dentists, dental technicians and their patients〉.

【訳】Dentistry 4 US Weekly紙は、歯科医、歯科技工士およびその患者の間では州内最大の発行部数を持つ。

- □ publication　名出版
- □ dentist　名歯科医
- □ realization　名認識
- □ dental technician　名歯科技工士
- □ notification　名通知

40. 正解 (D)

【解説】「平均以上の勝率を上げる」という後半の内容から考えて、keep up（保つ）の目的語として適当なのはreputation（名声）。

【構造】Lawyers (S) 〈at Jones & Simpson〉 keep up (V) the reputation (O) 〈of the firm〉 (by [maintaining a higher than average win percentage 〈for all their cases〉]).

【訳】Jones & Simpson社の弁護士たちは、すべての訴訟において平均以上の勝率を維持することによって事務所の名声を保っている。

- □ issue　名発行
- □ case　名訴訟
- □ memorandum　名メモ
- □ contrast　名対比

Lesson 6

意味や用法が適した**動詞の選択**
まぎらわしい・日本語と非対応なものに注意！

英語の動詞や動詞句も日本語とは非対応のものが多くあります。

たとえば、日本語では「借りる／貸す」といっても、英語では様々な状況に応じて言葉を使い分けます。これらを状況に応じて使いこなす力を試すのがこのタイプの問題です。また、ただ単に見かけがまぎらわしい動詞の判別を試す場合もあります。

例題： Because somebody took the extension cord from his cubicle, Jim had to ask a colleague to ------- one to him.

(A) borrow　　(B) lend　　(C) rent　　(D) loan

正解　**(B)**

訳　誰かが延長コードを彼のブースから持っていったので、ジムは同僚に貸してくれと頼まなければならなかった。

【解説】(A)borrowは「借りる」という意味なので、貸借関係が逆になります。また、同僚に有料で延長コードを貸すとは普通考えられないので、(C)rentも違います。(D)loanは「お金を貸す」という意味なので、当てはまりません。ここでは「貸す」という意味の(B)lendを選びます。

意味がまぎらわしい動詞の例「貸借する」

- ☐ borrow　　移動できる物を無料で借りる；お金を借りる
- ☐ lend　　　移動できる物を無料で貸す；お金を貸す
- ☐ use　　　 移動できないものをその場で借用する
- ☐ rent　　　料金を払って借りる；料金を取って貸す
- ☐ loan　　　お金を貸す

さて次に、動詞や動詞句の選択の問題です。

> 例題：Because of the heavy snowfall all over the area, the event organizers didn't have any choice but to -------- off the fair.
> (A) call　　(B) get　　(C) show　　(D) take

正解　**(A)**

訳　地域全域におよぶ大雪のため、イベント管理者たちは見本市を中止せざるを得なかった。

【解説】基本動詞と前置詞や副詞が組み合わされた英語表現は大変多くあり、よく使用されます。(B)get off は「降りる」、(C)show off は「見せびらかす」、(D)take off は「脱ぐ；離陸する」という意味なので、どれもこの文脈に当てはまりません。(A)call off（中止する）だと、前後の意味にぴったりです。

まぎらわしい動詞句の例「off を使ったもの」

- □ put off　　延期する（他動詞として＝postpone）
- □ call off　　中止する（他動詞として＝cancel）
- □ get off　　降ろす（他動詞として）；降りる（自動詞として）
- □ take off　　離陸する（自動詞として）；服などを脱ぐ（他動詞として）
- □ show off　　見せびらかす（他動詞、自動詞として）
- □ go off　　消える（自動詞として）
- □ come off　　とれる（自動詞として）

動詞を学ぶ際には、意味だけでなくそれらがどのような使われ方をするのか、その語法に留意しながら、例文と共に学ぶことも重要です。

EXERCISES

空所補充：各文を完全な形にするために、必要な語句を1つだけ選んでください。

1. Mr. Sang's briefcase simply ------- apart after over 16 years of heavy use.
   (A) took
   (B) grew
   (C) fell
   (D) got

2. Ms. Perez's supervisor called her into the office to ------- problems on the Vancouver contract.
   (A) resolve
   (B) charge
   (C) assist
   (D) revert

3. The Washington Natural Bagel Co. always ------- freshly baked goods from the finest organic ingredients.
   (A) amounts
   (B) creates
   (C) determines
   (D) tastes

4. Ms. Yamamoto had to first ------- the photographs on her desk into digital files so she could use them on her PC.
   (A) include
   (B) confer
   (C) convert
   (D) promote

全部で40問あります。1問20秒、13分20秒での完答を目指して挑戦しましょう。
すべて解答してから＜正解と解説＞と照合してください。

1. 正解 (C)

【解説】空所の後ろのapartと結びついて自動詞句を作る動詞を考え、空所にはfellを入れる。fall apartは「ばらばら［こなごな］に壊れる；崩壊する」という意味。

構造 Mr. Sang's briefcase ⓢ (simply) fell apart ⓥ (after over 16 years) 〈of heavy use〉.

【訳】Sang氏の書類かばんは、16年以上も酷使した末にあっさりバラバラになった。
□ briefcase ⓝ書類かばん　　□ fall apart ⓗばらばらなる　　□ heavy ⓐ激しい

2. 正解 (A)

【解説】problems（問題）を目的語に取る動詞として適当なのはresolve（解決する）。assistはhelpの同意語だから、人間を目的語にしてassist her with problemsのように言うのが正しい。

構造 Ms. Perez's supervisor ⓢ called ⓥ her ⓞ (into the office) (to resolve problems) 〈on the Vancouver contract〉.

【訳】Perez氏の上司は、バンクーバーの契約に関する諸問題を解決するために彼女を事務所に呼び入れた。
□ charge ⓥ請求する　　□ assist ⓥ助ける　　□ revert ⓥ戻る

3. 正解 (B)

【解説】bagelは米国で一般的なパンの一種で、freshly baked goodsとは「焼きたて品（ベーグル）」のこと。これを目的語とする動詞としては、creates（作り出す）が適当。

構造 The Washington Natural Bagel Co. ⓢ (always) creates ⓥ freshly baked goods ⓞ (from the finest organic ingredients).

【訳】Washington Natural Bagel社は、最高の有機食材を使っていつでも焼きたての品を作っている。
□ amounts ⓥ総計～に達する　　□ determines ⓥ決心する　　□ tastes ⓥ味わう
□ freshly baked ⓐ焼きたての　　□ organic ⓐ有機栽培の　　□ ingredient ⓝ材料

4. 正解 (C)

【解説】後ろのintoに着目して、convert A into B（AをBに変換する）という形を使う。他の選択肢は、「写真」を目的語にするには意味的に不自然。

構造 Ms. Yamamoto ⓢ had to (first) convert ⓥ the photographs ⓞ 〈on her desk〉 (into digital files) (so she could use them (on her PC)).

【訳】Yamamoto氏は、机の上の写真をパソコン上で使えるように最初にデジタルファイルに変換しなければならなかった。
□ include ⓥ含む　　□ confer ⓥ授与する　　□ promote ⓥ昇進させる；販売促進する

意味や用法が適した動詞の選択

5. Vice-president Achebe asked Ms. Sisulu to ------- notes at the meeting later that afternoon.
   (A) turn
   (B) ask
   (C) go
   (D) take

   Ⓐ Ⓑ Ⓒ Ⓓ

6. Housekeeping staff need at least three hours to ------- up rooms to receive new guests after previous ones have left.
   (A) hand
   (B) find
   (C) come
   (D) set

   Ⓐ Ⓑ Ⓒ Ⓓ

7. Ugo Industries ------- the equipment it needed from a supplier for two years before buying its own.
   (A) involved
   (B) contracted
   (C) agreed
   (D) impacted

   Ⓐ Ⓑ Ⓒ Ⓓ

8. Ms. Isaacs had to develop a very in-depth presentation to ------- across her main points to the client.
   (A) get
   (B) give
   (C) ask
   (D) keep

   Ⓐ Ⓑ Ⓒ Ⓓ

5. 正解 (D)

【解説】take [make] notes で「メモを取る」という意味の慣用表現になる。note は「メモ」の意味で、日本語の「ノート」に当たる語は notebook。

構造 Vice-president Achebe ⒮ asked ⓥ Ms. Sisulu ⓞ to take notes (at the meeting) (later that afternoon).

【訳】Achebe 副社長は、その日の午後の会議でメモを取るよう Sisulu 氏に頼んだ。

☐ turn 動回す　　　　　　☐ ask 動尋ねる　　　　　　☐ go 動行く

6. 正解 (D)

【解説】up と結びついて rooms を目的語に取る動詞を考えると、空所には set を入れるのが適当。set up a room で「部屋を設営する；整える」の意味を表す。

構造 Housekeeping staff ⒮ need ⓥ (at least) three hours ⓞ (to set up rooms) (to receive new guests) (after previous ones have left).

【訳】客室清掃スタッフは、前の客が出た後で新しい客を受け入れるために部屋を整えるのに少なくとも3時間を必要とする。

☐ housekeeping 名客室清掃　　☐ at least 熟少なくとも　　☐ set up 熟準備する
☐ receive 動迎える　　　　　☐ previous 形以前の

7. 正解 (B)

【解説】目的語が the equipment (備品) であることを考えると、その前に置いて意味の通る動詞は contract (契約する) の過去形、contracted (契約した；外注した) しか考えられない。

構造 Ugo Industries ⒮ contracted ⓥ the equipment ⓞ ⟨it needed⟩ (from a supplier) (for two years) (before buying its own).

【訳】Ugo Industries は、必要な備品を自社で購入する前は2年間業者から仕入れていた。

☐ involved involve の過去(分詞)形　☐ agreed agree の過去(分詞)形　☐ impacted impact の過去(分詞)形
☐ supplier 名納入業者

8. 正解 (A)

【解説】空所の後ろの across と結びついて意味をなすのは get のみ。get across A to B は「A を B に理解させる；伝える」という意味のイディオム。

構造 Ms. Isaacs ⒮ had to develop ⓥ a very in-depth presentation ⓞ (to get across her main points (to the client)).

【訳】Isaacs 氏は、依頼主に要点を理解させるために非常に詳細なプレゼンテーションを展開せねばならなかった。

☐ in-depth 形綿密な

9. Mr. Salome stopped by the studio on the way to ------- up the photos of the office party.
   (A) take
   (B) pick
   (C) show
   (D) stand

   Ⓐ Ⓑ Ⓒ Ⓓ

10. Luxury handbag maker Lucci Inc. has ------- a sales increase of 7% since it launched a cheaper range of brands.
   (A) contested
   (B) experienced
   (C) filtered
   (D) interviewed

   Ⓐ Ⓑ Ⓒ Ⓓ

11. The IT director ------- out her plan to store all essential files in a special mainframe.
   (A) added
   (B) laid
   (C) went
   (D) looked

   Ⓐ Ⓑ Ⓒ Ⓓ

12. More savers are ------- for long-term savings plans of five years or more to profit from higher interest rates.
   (A) choosing
   (B) gaining
   (C) opting
   (D) benefitting

   Ⓐ Ⓑ Ⓒ Ⓓ

9. 正解 (B)

【解説】選択肢の動詞はそれぞれupと結びつけて使うことができるが、文脈に合うのはpick up。ここでは「(預けていたものを)引き取る」の意味を表す。

構造 Mr. Salome (s) stopped (v) (by the studio) (on the way) (to pick up the photos ⟨of the office party⟩).

【訳】Salome氏は職場のパーティーの写真を受け取るために途中でスタジオに立ち寄った。

☐ stop by 熟立ち寄る　　　☐ on the way 熟途中で

10. 正解 (B)

【解説】「売り上げの増加を〜」という文脈に合うのはhas experienced(経験してきた)。has recorded(記録してきた)なども使える。

構造 Luxury handbag maker Lucci Inc. (s) has experienced (v) a sales increase (o) ⟨of 7%⟩ (since it launched a cheaper range ⟨of brands⟩).

【訳】高級ハンドバッグメーカーのLucci社は、安い価格帯のブランドを発売して以来、売り上げを7%増やしている。

☐ contested　contestの過去(分詞)形　☐ filtered　filterの過去(分詞)形　☐ interviewed　interviewの過去(分詞)形
☐ luxury　形高級な　　　　　　　　☐ increase　名増加　　　　　　　　☐ launch　動始める

11. 正解 (B)

【解説】outと結びついてplanを目的語に取る動詞を考えると、空所にはlaidを入れるのが適当。lay outには「(計画を)立案する」の意味がある。

構造 The IT director (s) laid out (v) her plan (o) ⟨to store all essential files (in a special mainframe)⟩.

【訳】IT責任者は、すべての必須のファイルを特別な大型コンピュータに保存する計画を練った。

☐ added　addの過去(分詞)形　　　　☐ went　goの過去形　　　　　☐ looked　lookの過去(分詞)形
☐ store　動記憶装置に記憶させる　　☐ essential　形必須の　　　　☐ mainframe　名汎用コンピュータ

12. 正解 (C)

【解説】opt(選ぶ)はoption(選択)の動詞形で、opt for 〜で「〜を選ぶ」の意味を表す。higher interest ratesとは、預け入れ期間が長いほど定期預金の利子が高くなることを指す。

構造 More savers (s) are opting (v) for long-term savings plans ⟨of five years or more⟩ (to profit from higher interest rates).

【訳】より高い利率から利益を得るために、5年以上の長期にわたる貯蓄計画を選択する預金者が増えている。

☐ choosing　chooseの現在分詞形　☐ gaining　gainの現在分詞形　☐ benefitting　benefitの現在分詞形
☐ saver　名貯蓄家　　　　　　　　☐ savings　名貯金　　　　　　　☐ profit from 〜　熟〜から利益を得る
☐ interest rate　名利率

意味や用法が適した動詞の選択

13. Certain employees may ------- to receive reimbursements for work-related courses they take on or offline.
- (A) divide
- (B) expend
- (C) qualify
- (D) acquire

Ⓐ Ⓑ Ⓒ Ⓓ

14. The CEO will ------- the trainees after making a few introductory remarks about their new duties.
- (A) speak
- (B) propose
- (C) feature
- (D) dismiss

Ⓐ Ⓑ Ⓒ Ⓓ

15. You must ------- in your worksheet to your supervisor no later than the end of each workweek to receive your pay on time.
- (A) back
- (B) hand
- (C) leave
- (D) make

Ⓐ Ⓑ Ⓒ Ⓓ

16. Mr. Querioz ------- in his application for the job vacancy after reading about it in a company newsletter.
- (A) filed
- (B) broke
- (C) dropped
- (D) turned

Ⓐ Ⓑ Ⓒ Ⓓ

13. 正解 (C)

【解説】選択肢のうち、後ろに不定詞を置けるのはqualifyのみ。qualify to Vは「Vする資格がある」の意味を表す。

構造 Certain employees ⓢ may qualify ⓥ (to receive reimbursements 〈for work-related courses 〈they take on or offline〉〉).

【訳】オンラインまたはオフラインで受講する業務に関連する課程の費用払い戻しを受ける資格を、一定の社員は持っている。

- □ divide 動分ける
- □ expend 動費やす
- □ acquire 動習得する
- □ certain 形(ある)一定の
- □ reimbursement 名払い戻し
- □ work-related 形業務に関連した

14. 正解 (D)

【解説】speakやproposeの後ろに人間を置くときはtoが必要。dismissは「解雇する」ではなく「解散[散会]させる；行かせる」の意味で使えば、意味の通る文になる。

構造 The CEO ⓢ will dismiss ⓥ the trainees ⓞ (after [making a few introductory remarks 〈about their new duties〉]).

【訳】CEOは、研修生たちの新しい任務に関する2～3のコメントをした後で彼らを解散させるだろう。

- □ speak 動話す
- □ propose 動提案する
- □ feature 動特徴づける
- □ introductory remarks 名序言
- □ duty 名任務

15. 正解 (B)

【解説】後ろのinと結びついてyour worksheetを目的語に取る動詞を考えると、空所にはhandを入れるのが適当。hand inは「～を提出する」の意味を表す。

構造 You ⓢ must hand in ⓥ your worksheet ⓞ (to your supervisor)(no later than the end of each workweek)(to receive your pay (on time)).

【訳】給料を遅れずに受け取るためには、各週の勤務日数の終わりまでに上司に業務報告書を提出しなければならない。

- □ worksheet 名業務報告書
- □ workweek 名1週間の勤務(日数)
- □ on time 熟時間どおりに

16. 正解 (D)

【解説】inと結びついてapplicationを目的語に取る動詞を考えると、空所にはturnedを入れるのが適当。turn in は「提出する」の意味で、hand in、send inとも言う。

構造 Mr. Querioz ⓢ turned in ⓥ his application ⓞ 〈for the job vacancy〉(after [reading about it (in a company newsletter)]).

【訳】Querioz氏は求人について社内報で読んだ後、それに応募する書類を提出した。

- □ application 名申し込み
- □ newsletter 名社内報；会報

17. Mr. Hussein missed his flight because he had been ------- in traffic on the way to the airport.
   (A) stuck
   (B) fixed
   (C) forced
   (D) cut

18. After she had written the report, Ms. Dao later had to ------- it to account for new information.
   (A) incline
   (B) participate
   (C) amend
   (D) suggest

19. Data Bank 19 Inc. will ------- your information for you, relieving you of the need to own large numbers of servers.
   (A) manage
   (B) appoint
   (C) react
   (D) cause

20. Mr. Khan strongly ------- that the building security team would be improved by hiring several more guards.
   (A) implied
   (B) collected
   (C) supervised
   (D) organized

17. 正解　(A)

【解説】「飛行機に乗り遅れた」という内容から考えて、be stuck in traffic（渋滞で動けなくなる）とするのが適当。stickには「～を立ち往生させる」の意味がある。

構造 Mr. Hussein ⓢ missed ⓥ his flight ⓞ (because he had been stuck (in traffic) (on the way to the airport)).

【訳】Hussein氏は、空港へ行く途中で渋滞で動けなくなったために飛行機の便に乗り遅れた。

- □ fixed　fixの過去(分詞)形
- □ forced　forceの過去(分詞)形
- □ cut　cutの過去(分詞)形

18. 正解　(C)

【解説】「報告書を書いた後でそれを～する」という文脈に合うのはamend（修正する）。itはthe reportを指すので、suggest（提案する）では意味的に不自然。

構造 (After she had written the report), Ms. Dao ⓢ (later) had to amend ⓥ it ⓞ (to account for new information).

【訳】報告書を書いた後、Dao氏は新しい情報を説明するために後で修正しなければならなかった。

- □ incline　⑩気持ちが傾く
- □ participate　⑩参加する
- □ suggest　⑩提案する
- □ account for ～　⑳～を説明する

19. 正解　(A)

【解説】「あなたの情報をあなたに代わって～する」の空所に入る適当な動詞はmanage（管理する）。reactは自動詞で、「～に反応する」はreact to ～と言う。

構造 Data Bank 19 Inc. ⓢ will manage ⓥ your information ⓞ (for you), (relieving you of the need ⟨to own large numbers of servers⟩).

【訳】Data Bank 19社は貴社の情報の管理を代行し、貴社が多数のサーバーを所有する必要をなくします。

- □ appoint　⑩指名する
- □ relieve A of B　⑳AからBを取り除いて楽にしてやる
- □ react　⑩作用する
- □ own　⑩所有する
- □ cause　⑩原因となる
- □ server　⑳サーバー

20. 正解　(A)

【解説】後ろにthat節を置ける動詞は、think・know・sayなど思考、認識、発言に関連するものが多い。選択肢の中ではimply（暗示する）がそれに当たり、他の動詞は後ろにthat節を置けない。

構造 Mr. Khan ⓢ (strongly) implied ⓥ [ⓞ that the building security team would be improved (by [hiring several more guards])].

【訳】Khan氏は、ビル警備チームは守衛をもう数人雇えば改善されるだろうと強く示唆した。

- □ collected　collectの過去(分詞)形
- □ supervised　superviseの過去(分詞)形
- □ organized　organizeの過去(分詞)形
- □ strongly　⑩強く
- □ security　⑳警備
- □ guard　⑳守衛

意味や用法が適した動詞の選択

21. The deliverymen were able to ------- out the installation of Ms. Roche's new fridge freezer in only 35 minutes.
   (A) bring
   (B) push
   (C) carry
   (D) lift

22. Loss-prevention specialists are positioned at the entrances of the mall to ------- that no goods leave that have not been paid for.
   (A) protect
   (B) monitor
   (C) search
   (D) ensure

23. New legislation cutting taxes on commercial real estate by up to €300,000 has ------- building occupancy rates considerably in Brussels.
   (A) enticed
   (B) boosted
   (C) succeeded
   (D) represented

24. The issue of price ------- out the sales negotiations for an additional six weeks.
   (A) came
   (B) drew
   (C) made
   (D) let

21. 正解 (C)

【解説】選択肢の動詞はどれもoutと結びつけて使うことができるが、空所の後ろのinstallation（取り付け）との意味的なつながりから考えて、空所にはcarryを入れる。carry outは「～を実行する；行う」の意味。

構造 The deliverymen ⓢ were ⓥ able ⓒ to carry out the installation 〈of Ms. Roche's new fridge freezer〉 (in only 35 minutes).

【訳】配達員たちは、Roche氏の新しい冷凍冷蔵庫をわずか35分以内に取り付けることができた。

☐ deliveryman ⓝ 配達人　　　☐ installation ⓝ 取り付け　　　☐ fridge freezer ⓝ 冷凍冷蔵庫

22. 正解 (D)

【解説】意味の紛らわしい選択肢が並んでいるが、後ろにthat節を置けるのはensure（保証する；確実に～する）のみ。loss-prevention specialistsは、ここでは万引き防止の監視員のこと。

構造 Loss-prevention specialists ⓢ are positioned ⓥ (at the entrances 〈of the mall〉) (to ensure [that no goods leave 〈that have not been paid for〉]).

【訳】支払いの済んでいない商品が1つも出て行かないよう確認するために、損失防止の専門家たちがショッピングモールの入り口に配備されている。

☐ protect ⓥ 保護する　　　☐ monitor ⓥ 監視する　　　☐ search ⓥ 捜す
☐ prevention ⓝ 防止　　　☐ position ⓥ 置く　　　☐ entrance ⓝ 入口

23. 正解 (B)

【解説】税の削減が主語になっているので、「建物占有率を引き上げた（boosted）」とすれば意味の通る文が完成する。

構造 New legislation ⓢ 〈cutting taxes 〈on commercial real estate〉（by up to €300,000)〉 has boosted ⓥ building occupancy rates ⓞ (considerably) (in Brussels).

【訳】商業用不動産に課される税を最高30万ユーロまで削減する新しい法律は、ブリュッセルの建物占有率を著しく引き上げた。

☐ enticed　　enticeの過去（分詞）形　　☐ succeeded　　succeedの過去（分詞）形
☐ represented　representの過去（分詞）形　☐ legislation ⓝ 法律　　☐ real estate 不動産
☐ occupancy ⓝ 入居；占有　　　☐ considerably ⓐ かなり

24. 正解 (B)

【解説】outと結びついてnegotiationsを目的語に取る動詞を考えると、空所にはdrewを入れるのが適当。draw outは「～を引き伸ばす」の意味で使う。

構造 The issue ⓢ 〈of price〉 drew out ⓥ the sales negotiations ⓞ (for an additional six weeks).

【訳】価格の問題が商談をさらに6週間引き延ばした。

☐ issue ⓝ 問題　　　☐ negotiation ⓝ 交渉

意味や用法が適した動詞の選択

25. Ms. Akebe continued to bid on the auction item, although its rising price caused others to ------- out.
    (A) hand
    (B) drop
    (C) blow
    (D) force

26. The conference gave Ms. Dench several ideas about how to ------- her own team of sales representatives.
    (A) open
    (B) motivate
    (C) commence
    (D) correspond

27. Ladies visiting the store can now ------- a personal shopper to help them choose the perfect outfit.
    (A) consult
    (B) function
    (C) discount
    (D) prove

28. The expansion of Takahashi Co. led it to ------- its original headquarters in Kobe and relocate to Tokyo.
    (A) forward
    (B) schedule
    (C) outgrow
    (D) repeat

25. 正解 (B)

【解説】後ろのoutと結びついて自動詞句を作るのは、もともと自動詞であるdropとblow。blow out（爆発する）は文脈に合わないが、drop out（脱落する）なら意味が通る。

構造 Ms. Akebe ⓢ continued ⓥ [ⓞ to bid (on the auction item)], (although its rising price caused others to drop out).

【訳】値が上がって他の入札者は脱落したが、Akebe氏はその競売品を競り続けた。

☐ bid on ～ (熟)～に入札をする   ☐ cause ～ to V (熟)～にVさせる

26. 正解 (B)

【解説】openやcommenceの目的語はふつう事物であり、correspondは自動詞だから後ろに名詞は置けない。motivate（動機づける；やる気にさせる）が意味的に最も適当。

構造 The conference ⓢ gave ⓥ Ms. Dench ⓞ1 several ideas ⓞ2 〈about [how to motivate her own team] 〈of sales representatives〉]〉.

【訳】その会議からDench氏は、自身が管理する営業担当者チームの士気を高める方法についていくつかのアイデアを得た。

☐ open (動)開ける   ☐ commence (動)開始する   ☐ correspond (動)一致する
☐ how to V (熟)Vするための方法

27. 正解 (A)

【解説】選択肢のうち、人間を目的語にしたとき意味をなす動詞はconsult（相談する）のみ。personal shopperとは、本人の代わりに買い物をしてくれるスタッフのこと。

構造 Ladies ⓢ 〈visiting the store〉 can (now) consult ⓥ a personal shopper ⓞ 〈to help them choose the perfect outfit〉.

【訳】その店を訪れる女性客は、今なら買い物ヘルパーに相談して完璧な服装一式を選ぶ手伝いをしてもらえる。

☐ function (動)機能を果たす   ☐ discount (動)割り引く   ☐ prove (動)証明する
☐ personal shopper (名)買い物ヘルパー   ☐ outfit (名)服装一式

28. 正解 (C)

【解説】lead ～ to V は「～をVする結果に至らせる」の意味。ここではoutgrow（～より大きくなる）を空所に入れて「神戸の本社が手狭になったので東京へ移転した」という意味にするのが自然。

構造 The expansion ⓢ 〈of Takahashi Co.〉 led ⓥ it ⓞ to outgrow ⓒ1 its original headquarters 〈in Kobe〉 and relocate ⓒ2 (to Tokyo).

【訳】Takahashi社は成長して、神戸にあった元の本社が手狭になって東京へ移転した。

☐ forward (動)転送する   ☐ schedule (動)予定する   ☐ repeat (動)繰り返して言う
☐ lead ～ to V (熟)～にVする気にさせる   ☐ original (形)元の   ☐ headquarters (名)本社

29. Staff who ------- notable leadership skills may apply for the junior management program after 18 months of service with us.
　(A) believe
　(B) occur
　(C) come
　(D) show

30. The warehouse manager told the night staff to -------- on the lights in the upper storeroom at 7:00 A.M.
　(A) hold
　(B) switch
　(C) touch
　(D) press

31. Employees must ------- clear of sections of the factory that are neither within their work areas nor designated as public spaces.
　(A) take
　(B) start
　(C) stay
　(D) make

32. The PacificBusineses50.com article on trade ------- in with previous articles posted on the topic.
　(A) moves
　(B) lies
　(C) writes
　(D) ties

29. 正解 (D)

【解説】「指導力」を目的語に取る動詞として適当なのは show（示す）。occur や come は自動詞だから、後ろに名詞（目的語）を置くことはできない。

構造 Staff ⓢ ⟨who **show** notable leadership skills⟩ may apply ⓥ (for the junior management program) (after 18 months of service ⟨with us⟩).

【訳】卓越した指導力を示すスタッフは、当職場で18か月勤務した後に幹部補佐研修プログラムに申し込んでよい。

- □ believe　　　⑩信じる　　　　　□ occur　　⑩生じる　　　　□ come　　⑩来る
- □ notable　　　⑯卓越した　　　　□ skill　　⑳技能　　　　　□ apply for ～　⑰～に申し込む
- □ junior management　⑳幹部補佐　　□ service　⑳勤務

30. 正解 (B)

【解説】空所の後ろの on と結びついて the lights を目的語とする動詞としては、switch が適当。switch on [off] で「～のスイッチを入れる[消す]」の意味を表す。

構造 The warehouse manager ⓢ told ⓥ the night staff ⓞ to **switch** on the lights (in the upper storeroom) (at 7:00 A.M).

【訳】倉庫の管理者は、午前7時に上階の貯蔵室の明かりをつけるよう夜勤のスタッフに言った。

- □ storeroom　⑳貯蔵室

31. 正解 (C)

【解説】clear には「～から離れて」という意味があり、stay clear of ～で「～に近づかない」の意味を表す。この場合の stay は「～の状態でいる」の意味。

構造 Employees ⓢ must stay ⓥ **clear** ⓒ (of sections ⟨of the factory⟩ ⟨that are neither (within their work areas) nor designated (as public spaces)⟩⟩).

【訳】従業員は、自分の作業エリア内でもなく指定された公共スペースでもない工場内の区域に立ち入ってはならない。

- □ take　　　　　　⑩取る　　　　　　□ start　　　⑩出発する　　　□ make　　　⑩作る
- □ neither A nor B　⑳AでもBでもない　□ work area　⑳作業エリア　　□ designate　⑩指定する
- □ public space　　⑳公共スペース

32. 正解 (D)

【解説】空所の後ろの in with に着目して、空所には tie を入れる。tie in with ～は「～と結びついている」の意味。

構造 The PacificBusineses50.com article ⓢ ⟨on trade⟩ **ties** in ⓥ (with previous articles ⟨posted on the topic⟩).

【訳】PacificBusineses50.com の商業に関する記事は、その話題に関して掲載された以前の記事と結びついている。

- □ article　⑳記事　　　　　　□ trade　⑳商業　　　　　□ post　⑩掲載する
- □ topic　　⑳話題

意味や用法が適した動詞の選択

33. Mr. Phelps was persuaded to ------- over to a rival corporation after it offered him a 22% increase on his current salary.
   (A) cross
   (B) put
   (C) stand
   (D) let

   Ⓐ Ⓑ Ⓒ Ⓓ

34. Assam Airline passengers are asked to ------- the check-in counter if they require vegetarian in-flight meals.
   (A) confirm
   (B) confess
   (C) inform
   (D) state

   Ⓐ Ⓑ Ⓒ Ⓓ

35. Many supermarkets now ------- food items with their sugar and sodium content.
   (A) label
   (B) look
   (C) print
   (D) view

   Ⓐ Ⓑ Ⓒ Ⓓ

36. Mr. Aseveda spent the afternoon ------- through the file cabinet searching for several documents he needed.
   (A) sorting
   (B) coming
   (C) pointing
   (D) trying

   Ⓐ Ⓑ Ⓒ Ⓓ

33. 正解　(A)

【解説】空所の後ろのoverとの結びつきを考慮して文意を考え、空所にはcrossを入れる。cross overは「転身する、(敵側へ)寝返る」の意味。

構造 Mr. Phelps (S) was persuaded (V) to cross over (to a rival corporation) (after it offered him a 22% increase) ⟨on his current salary⟩).

【訳】Phelps氏は、22%の昇給をライバル社から提示された後で同社に移るよう説得された。

- □ persuade 〜 to V　(熟)〜を説得してVさせる
- □ salary　(名)給料

34. 正解　(C)

【解説】目的語としてどんな名詞が後ろに来るかを考えると、confirmは「予約」など、confessは「過ち」など、stateは「意見」など。ここではinform (知らせる) を選んで「搭乗受付カウンターに知らせる」とするのが意味的に最も自然。

構造 Assam Airline passengers (S) are asked (V) to inform the check-in counter (if they require vegetarian in-flight meals).

【訳】Assam航空にご搭乗のお客様で、機内での菜食料理をご希望の場合は搭乗受付カウンターにお知らせください。

- □ confirm　(動)確かめる
- □ confess　(動)白状する
- □ state　(動)述べる
- □ vegetarian　(形)菜食主義の
- □ in-flight　(形)飛行中の

35. 正解　(A)

【解説】後ろのwithに着目して、label A with B (AにBのラベルを貼る) という形を作る。「食品を印刷する」や「食品を見る」は意味的に不自然。

構造 Many supermarkets (S) (now) label (V) food items (O) (with their sugar and sodium content).

【訳】現在では多くのスーパーマーケットが、糖分と塩化ナトリウムの含有量を示すラベルを食品に貼っている。

- □ look　(動)見る
- □ print　(動)印刷する
- □ view　(動)見る
- □ sodium　(名)ナトリウム
- □ content　(名)含有量

36. 正解　(A)

【解説】空所の後ろのthroughとの結びつきから考えて、空所にはsortingを入れる。sort throughは「〜をかき分けて調べる」の意味。

構造 Mr. Aseveda (S) spent (V) the afternoon (O) (sorting through the file cabinet) (searching for several documents ⟨he needed⟩).

【訳】Aseveda氏は、書類整理棚をかき分けながら必要とするいくつかの書類を探して午後を過ごした。

- □ file cabinet　(名)書類整理棚
- □ search for 〜　(熟)〜を探す

意味や用法が適した動詞の選択

37. The article about CEO Thomas Rai may ------- in the next edition of the Times of South Asia.
    (A) appear
    (B) mail
    (C) subscribe
    (D) distribute

38. Mr. Al-Zayyat ordinarily likes to ------- the data in his subordinates' reports before arranging department meetings to discuss it.
    (A) caution
    (B) operate
    (C) respond
    (D) review

39. Mr. O'Leary plans to ------- the planning department with WorkSmart tables and chairs as they are economical, stylish and easy to put together.
    (A) build
    (B) resort
    (C) assemble
    (D) furnish

40. Although he often flew on business trips, Mr. Khasani still became a little anxious when the plane was about to ------- off.
    (A) take
    (B) rise
    (C) wear
    (D) turn

37. 正解　(A)

【解説】選択肢のうちで自動詞として使うのはappear（現れる）のみ。appearは「（新聞に）載る」「（テレビに）出る」などの場合にも使う。

構造　The article ⓢ ⟨about CEO Thomas Rai⟩ may appear ⓥ (in the next edition) ⟨of the Times of South Asia⟩).

【訳】CEOのThomas Rai氏に関する記事が、Times of South Asiaの次の版に出るかもしれない。

- □ mail　　　働郵送する
- □ subscribe　働購読する
- □ distribute　働分配する

38. 正解　(D)

【解説】review the data（データを見直す）が意味的に最も自然。cautionは人間を目的語に取る。operate the dataは意味的に不自然。respondは自動詞なので、後ろに名詞を置くときはtoが必要。

構造　Mr. Al-Zayyat ⓢ (ordinarily) likes ⓥ [ⓞ to review the data ⟨in his subordinates' reports⟩] (before arranging department meetings ⟨to discuss it⟩).

【訳】Al-Zayyat氏はふだん、部下の報告のデータを議論する部内会議を手配する前にそれを見直したがる。

- □ caution　　働警告を与える
- □ operate　働作動する
- □ respond　働返答する
- □ ordinarily　働通常
- □ subordinate　图部下
- □ arrange　働手配する

39. 正解　(D)

【解説】後ろのwithに着目して、furnish A with B（AにBを備え付ける）という形を作れば意味の通る文になる。同意語のequipも、この形で使える。

構造　Mr. O'Leary ⓢ plans ⓥ [ⓞ to furnish the planning department (with WorkSmart tables and chairs)] (as they are economical, stylish and easy (to put together)).

【訳】O' Leary氏は、経済的で品がよく、また組み立てやすいWorkSmart社製のテーブルといすを企画部に備え付ける予定だ。

- □ build　　　　働建てる
- □ resort　　　働訴える
- □ assemble　働集める
- □ planning department　图企画部
- □ economical　形経済的な
- □ stylish　形上品な
- □ put together　熟組み立てる

40. 正解　(A)

【解説】主語が飛行機なので、空所にはtakeを入れる。take offは「離陸する」。wear off（徐々に消える；すり減らす）もよく使うイディオム。

構造　(Although he often flew (on business trips)), Mr. Khasani ⓢ (still) became ⓥ a little anxious ⓒ (when the plane was about to take off).

【訳】飛行機で出張することがよくあるけれど、Khasani氏は飛行機がまさに離陸しようとした時にはまだ少し不安になった。

- □ business trip　图出張
- □ anxious　形不安な
- □ be about to V　熟Vしようとしている

意味や用法が適した動詞の選択

Lesson 7 意味や用法が適した接続詞・前置詞・論理マーカーの選択
熟語増強や前後の文脈からの読み取り！

　接続詞、前置詞などの接続要素を選択させるタイプの問題です。
　これらには、**形式的な選択**をさせるもの、**意味的な選択**をさせるものがあります。また**イディオムの一部となっている前置詞を選ぶ**問題もあります。典型的な問題を見ながら、対策を考えてみましょう。

例題：At the press conference, Mr. Green spoke as the representative of the company, saying that ------- the heavy drop in profits, it wouldn't slow production.

(A) though　　(B) in spite of　　(C) in favor of　　(D) however

正解　**(B)**

訳　記者会見において、グリーン氏は会社の代表として、利益の大幅な低下にもかかわらず、減産は行わないと述べた。

【解説】形式的な面からは、空所の直後には名詞句があるので、前置詞の働きをするものが選択されると考え、(A)though（接続詞）、(D)however（接続副詞）をカットすることができます。また、意味的な側面からは、直後にネガティブな要素が置かれ、主節がポジティブな意味となっているため、逆接の意味を持ったものが入ると考えられ、(C)in favor of（～に賛成して）ではなく、(B)in spite of（～にもかかわらず）を選びます。

◎接続詞と前置詞でまぎらわしいもの

while S V	（SがVする間、一方で）	→接続詞
during ～	（～の間）	→前置詞
though S V	（SはVするけれども）	→接続詞
in spite of ～	（～にもかかわらず）＝despite ～	→前置詞

意味と形式の両方の視点を持ち、選択肢を判別していきましょう。

次に単体の前置詞を選択する問題を見てみましょう。

例題： To avoid the risk of customers' personal information leaking out of the company, the supervisor asked the employees to dispose ------- the documents in the proper manner.
(A) of   (B) with   (C) at   (D) to

正解 **(A)**

訳 顧客の個人情報が会社から漏れるのを防ぐため、管理者は従業員に書類を適切な方法で処分するよう指示した。

【解説】他動詞句の一部となっている前置詞を選択する問題（dispose of 〜は「〜を処分する」という意味）。前置詞の原義を考えて答えられる問題とも言い難いので、やはりこのような熟語は普段から増強する必要があります。

次に、Part 6 でも出題の可能性が高い、論理マーカー（文と文との間に位置し、それらを様々な意味の流れで連結するもの）の判別について見てみましょう。

例題：The annual profit of ZX Corporation has declined by 40 percent. -------, it is expected that the market will be slow until the end of next year.
(A) Therefore   (B) However   (C) Besides   (D) Briefly

正解 **(C)**

訳 ZX 社の年間の売り上げは 40 パーセント低下している。それに加えて来年末まで市場は低調だと予測されている。

【解説】前半の文では「① ZX 社の売り上げが低下しているという事実」、後半の文では「②市場の低調は継続するという見通し」が述べられています。これらは同じ方向性の内容（逆接ではない）ので、(B)However（しかしながら）は答えにはなりません。また、①が②の理由となるわけではないので、(A)Therefore（それ故に）も違います。また、②は①を要約しているわけでもないので、(D)Briefly（要するに）も答えにはなりません。①に②を追加する場合に使う、(C)Besides（さらに）が正解となります。

論理マーカーは、**前後の文の意味の関係**によって見抜くことができます。
なお 169 ページに一覧を設けましたので、あわせて参照ください。

意味や用法が適した接続詞・前置詞・論理マーカーの選択

EXERCISES

空所補充：各文を完全な形にするために、必要な語句を1つだけ選んでください。

1. Not surprisingly, ice cream purchases are at their highest ------- summer, particularly the month of August.
   (A) at
   (B) in
   (C) on
   (D) of

2. A detour road across Lexington Street was opened ------- motorists could still access the main shopping area downtown.
   (A) beyond
   (B) but that
   (C) so that
   (D) either

3. Users are warned against exceeding the recommended dosage; -------, the company assumes no liability for misuse of this medicine.
   (A) consequently
   (B) the moment
   (C) now that
   (D) whenever

4. The consignment of orange juice arrived ------- Sun Bay Supermarket's receiving areas had opened for the day.
   (A) both
   (B) either
   (C) for
   (D) before

全部で40問あります。1問20秒、13分20秒での完答を目指して挑戦しましょう。
すべて解答してから＜正解と解説＞と照合してください。

1. 正解　(B)
【解説】季節や月の前に置く前置詞はin。in summerで「夏に」の意味を表す。日付の前にはon、時刻の前にはatを使う。

構造 (Not surprisingly), ice cream purchases ⓢ are ⓥ at their highest ⓒ (in summer, (particularly) the month ⟨of August⟩).

【訳】驚くことではないが、アイスクリームの購入は夏場、特に8月が最高である。

☐ surprisingly　副驚いたことに　　☐ purchase　名購入　　　　☐ particularly　副特に

2. 正解　(C)
【解説】空所の後ろが完全な文の形なので、空所には接続詞が入る。後ろのcouldとの結びつきを考えて、so that ～ can V（～がVできるように）の形にすればよい。

構造 A detour road ⓢ ⟨across Lexington Street⟩ was opened ⓥ (so that motorists could still access the main shopping area downtown).

【訳】繁華街の主要商店街へ車でも行けるよう、レキシントン通りの向かいに迂回路が開通した。

☐ beyond　前～の向こうに　　　　☐ either　形どちらかの　　　　☐ detour　名迂回路
☐ motorist　名自動車を乗り回す人

3. 正解　(A)
【解説】空所の前のセミコロンは、カンマよりも強い（ピリオドに近い）区切りを表す。空所の後ろにもカンマがあるので、空所には副詞のconsequently（その結果；そういう事情で）を入れる。

構造 Users ⓢ are warned ⓥ (against exceeding the recommended dosage); (consequently), the company ⓢ assumes ⓥ no liability ⓒ ⟨for misuse ⟨of this medicine⟩⟩.

【訳】利用者は推奨される服用量を超えないようご注意ください。したがって、当社はこの薬の誤用に対する責任を負いません。

☐ the moment　接.....するやいなや　☐ now that　接今や.....だから　☐ whenever　接.....するときはいつでも
☐ exceed　動超える　　　　　　　☐ recommended　形推薦できる　　☐ dosage　名服用量
☐ assume　動（責任を）取る　　　☐ liability　名責任　　　　　　　☐ misuse　名誤用

4. 正解　(D)
【解説】空所の後ろが完全な文の形であり、時制が過去完了形（had opened）になっている点に着目して、接続詞のbefore（.....する前に）を入れる。

構造 The consignment ⓢ ⟨of orange juice⟩ arrived ⓥ (before Sun Bay Supermarket's receiving areas had opened (for the day)).

【訳】Sun Bay Supermarketの受け入れエリアがその日に開く前に、オレンジジュースの委託貨物が届いた。

☐ both　形両方の　　　　　☐ either　接.....か.....　　　　☐ for　接というわけは.....だから
☐ consignment　名委託貨物　☐ receiving area　名受け入れエリア

意味や用法が適した接続詞・前置詞・論理マーカーの選択

5. Elevators on this wall will not stop at floors 12 ------- 15 while repair work is being carried out.
   (A) however
   (B) in which
   (C) through
   (D) in terms of

6. Professor Krishna's seminar, ------, reviewed some of the most advanced theories in e-commerce systems.
   (A) to the extent that
   (B) for
   (C) until
   (D) in brief

7. Production staff were asked to work overtime ------- the recent labor shortage.
   (A) through
   (B) close to
   (C) owing to
   (D) except for

8. ------- the Bureau of Labor Statistics, the mean annual wage for construction workers in July 2009 was slightly lower than that of the last year.
   (A) Instead of
   (B) According
   (C) Instead
   (D) According to

5. 正解 (C)

【解説】while以下を取り外して考えると、at floors 12 through 15（12階から15階までに）という形にすれば意味が通るとわかる。

構造 Elevators ⓢ ⟨on this wall⟩ will not stop ⓥ (at floors 12 through 15) (while repair work is being carried out).

【訳】この壁のエレベーターは、修理が行われている間は12階から15階まで止まりません。

☐ however　副しかしながら　　　☐ in terms of ～　熟～の点から

6. 正解 (D)

【解説】空所に入る語句を取り外しても文が成り立つので、空所には修飾語（副詞）の働きをする in brief（要するに）を入れる。

構造 Professor Krishna's seminar ⓢ, (in brief), reviewed ⓥ some ⓞ ⟨of the most advanced theories ⟨in e-commerce systems⟩⟩.

【訳】Krishna教授のゼミは、手短に言えば、電子商取引システムにおける最先端の理論のいくつかを概説するものだった。

☐ to the extent that　接……という点程度まで　☐ for　接というわけは……だから　☐ until　前～まで
☐ review　動概説する　　　　　　　　　　　　☐ advanced　形先進の　　　　　　　　　　☐ theory　名理論
☐ e-commerce　名電子商取引

7. 正解 (C)

【解説】空所の後ろは名詞句なので、空所には前置詞に相当する語句が入る。意味から考えて、owing to ～（～のために）が適当。

構造 Production staff ⓢ were asked ⓥ to work (overtime) (owing to the recent labor shortage).

【訳】最近の労働力不足のために、生産スタッフは残業するよう依頼された。

☐ through　前～を通して　　　☐ close to ～　熟～に近い　　☐ except for　熟～は別として
☐ overtime　副時間外に　　　☐ recent　形最近の　　　　　☐ labor shortage　名労働力不足

8. 正解 (D)

【解説】情報源を目的語として「～によれば」という場合にはaccording to ～という前置詞句を用いる。instead of ～は「～の代わりに」という意味なので、文意に合わない。

構造 (According to the Bureau of Labor Statistics), the mean annual wage ⓢ ⟨for construction workers in July 2009⟩ was ⓥ slightly lower ⓒ (than that ⟨of the last year⟩).

【訳】労働統計局によれば、2009年の7月の建設労働者の平均年収は前年度よりもわずかに低下した。

☐ the Bureau of Labor Statistics　名労働統計局　　☐ mean　形平均の
☐ annual wage　名年収　　　　　　　　　　　　　☐ slightly　副わずかに

9. Beachwear Inc. lowered their operating costs by 15% ------- their competitors were unable to do the same.
   (A) while
   (B) then
   (C) in that
   (D) is concerned

10. BuyRCanada.com receives thousands of visits every day, ------- less than half of them are ultimately converted into sales.
   (A) even though
   (B) in order to
   (C) as for
   (D) not only

11. After a year of working at the corporation, Ms. O'Callaghan was offered stock options ------- those included in her current employee benefits.
   (A) around to
   (B) beyond
   (C) in definition of
   (D) in reaction to

12. Ms. Rossellini attended the meeting through a video link ------- she was too busy to fly over.
   (A) due
   (B) because
   (C) so
   (D) owing

9. 正解 (A)

【解説】空所の後ろが完全な文なので、空所には接続詞が入る。前後の内容が対比されていると考えて、空所にはwhile（ところが一方では……）を入れるのが適当。

構造 Beachwear Inc.ⓢ loweredⓥ their operating costsⓞ (by 15%) (while their competitors were unable to do the same).

【訳】Beachwear社は営業費を15％削減したが、競合他社には同じことはできなかった。

☐ then 　副 それから　　☐ in that 　接 ……という点で　　☐ operating costs 　名 営業費
☐ competitor 　名 競争相手

10. 正解 (A)

【解説】空所の後ろが完全な文の形なので、空所には接続詞が入る。選択肢のうち接続詞はeven though（たとえ……でも；……だけれど）のみであり、これを入れると意味が通じる文になる。

構造 BuyRCanada.comⓢ receivesⓥ thousands of visitsⓞ (every day), (even though less than half ⟨of them⟩ are (ultimately) converted (into sales)).

【訳】BuyRCanada.comには毎日何千ものアクセスがある。最終的に売り上げに転化するものはそのうち半分にも満たないが。

☐ in order to V 　熟 Vするために　　☐ as for ～ 　熟 ～について言えば　　☐ not only A but B 　熟 AばかりでなくBも
☐ ultimately 　副 最終的に　　☐ convert A into B 　熟 AをBに変える

11. 正解 (B)

【解説】空所の後ろのthoseは直前のstock optionsを受ける代名詞と考え、空所にはbeyond（～を越えて）を入れると意味の通る文が完成する。

構造 (After a year of working (at the corporation)), Ms. O'Callaghanⓢ was offeredⓥ stock options ⟨beyond those ⟨included (in her current employee benefits)⟩⟩.

【訳】その会社に1年勤めた後、O'Callaghan氏は現行の社員手当に含まれる以上の自社株購入権を提供された。

☐ stock option 　名 自社株購入権　　☐ include 　動 含む　　☐ benefit 　名 給付

12. 正解 (B)

【解説】空所の後ろが完全な文の形なので、接続詞のbecauseとsoのどちらかが入る。後半が前半の理由になっているので、because（……なので）を入れるのが適当。

構造 Ms. Rosselliniⓢ attendedⓥ the meetingⓞ (through a video link) (because she was too busy (to fly over)).

【訳】Rossellini氏は、多忙のため飛行機で出向くことができなかったので、テレビ電話を通じて会議に出席した。

☐ due 　形 支払期限の来た　　☐ so 　接 だから　　☐ owing 　形 未払いの
☐ video link 　名 テレビ会議システムによる接続

13. Come in to our downtown store to see discounts exclusively available ------- our summer sale.
    (A) when
    (B) during
    (C) along
    (D) as   Ⓐ Ⓑ Ⓒ Ⓓ

14. Because Mr. Faja was ------- pressure to complete his project, he told his assistant to hold all his calls.
    (A) along
    (B) within
    (C) under
    (D) behind   Ⓐ Ⓑ Ⓒ Ⓓ

15. All visitors to this site must wear hardhats and protective goggles ------- commercial safety regulations.
    (A) in accordance with
    (B) for the benefit of
    (C) as concerning
    (D) by means of   Ⓐ Ⓑ Ⓒ Ⓓ

16. Mr. Prajeuski's pay raise was a surprise ------- the fact that he had only been at the Warsaw branch a few months.
    (A) because
    (B) although
    (C) given
    (D) since   Ⓐ Ⓑ Ⓒ Ⓓ

13. 正解 (B)

【解説】空所の後ろは名詞句なので、空所には前置詞が入る。前後の文脈から考えて、during (〜の間に) を入れるのが適当。

構造 Come in (to our downtown store) (to see discounts ⟨(exclusively) available (during our summer sale)⟩).

【訳】繁華街の当店にお入りいただき、夏の特売期間限定でご利用いただける安売りをご覧ください。

- □ when 　接 ..... するとき
- □ along 　前 〜に沿って
- □ as 　前 〜として
- □ downtown 　名 繁華街
- □ exclusively 　副 全く..... のみ

14. 正解 (C)

【解説】空所の後ろのpressureと結びつく前置詞はunder (〜を受けて)。under pressureで「重圧下にある；プレッシャーを受けている」という意味を表す。

構造 (Because Mr. Faja was under pressure ⟨to complete his project⟩), he told his assistant to hold all his calls.

【訳】Faja氏は課題を完成させる重圧を受けていたので、自分あての電話はすべて取りつがないよう助手に言った。

- □ along 　前 〜に沿って
- □ within 　前 〜の内部に
- □ behind 　前 〜の後ろに
- □ pressure 　名 重圧
- □ complete 　動 完成させる
- □ hold 　動 引き留めておく

15. 正解 (A)

【解説】空所の前が「来訪者は〜しなければならない」という内容なので、空所にはin accordance with 〜 (〜に従って) を入れて「安全規制に従って」とすれば意味が通る文になる。

構造 All visitors ⟨to this site⟩ must wear hardhats and protective goggles (in accordance with commercial safety regulations).

【訳】この敷地への来訪者はすべて、業務用の安全規定に従って、ヘルメットと防護用ゴーグルを着用しなければならない。

- □ for the benefit of 〜 　熟 〜のために
- □ by means of 〜 　熟 〜の手段によって
- □ site 　名 敷地
- □ hardhat 　名 ヘルメット
- □ protective 　形 保護用の
- □ goggle 　名 ゴーグル
- □ commercial 　形 業務用の
- □ safety regulations 　名 安全規定

16. 正解 (C)

【解説】the fact以下は「〜という事実」という名詞の働きをする。その前には前置詞を置く必要があり、意味から考えてgiven (〜と仮定すると；〜を考えれば) を入れるのが適当。

構造 Mr. Prajeuski's pay raise was a surprise, (given the fact ⟨that he had only been (at the Warsaw branch) (a few months)⟩).

【訳】Prajeuski氏がワルシャワ支店に来てほんの数ヶ月だという事実を考えると、彼の昇給は意外だった。

- □ because 　接 ..... なので
- □ although 　接 ..... だけれども
- □ since 　接 ..... して以来
- □ surprise 　名 意外な事

17. Mr. Achmed felt the investment proposals were reasonable; ------- he had reached no final decision on them.
(A) furthermore
(B) on the other hand
(C) in case
(D) in order that

18. The keynote address at the conference will be ------- the impact of online advertisements in global markets.
(A) of
(B) to
(C) around
(D) about

19. Mr. Gupta said he was ready to dismiss the conferees, ------- any last questions participants might have had.
(A) once
(B) apart from
(C) whereupon
(D) by reason of

20. According to media reports, Kuanda Inc. will hire an additional 550 workers, ------- product demand continues to increase at present rates.
(A) so much so
(B) beyond which
(C) assuming that
(D) rather than

17. 正解 (B)

【解説】前半の「提案は理にかなっていた」と後半の「最終決定に至っていない」は対立する内容だから、on the other hand（他方では）を入れると意味が通じる。

構造 Mr. Achmed ⓢ felt ⓥ [ⓞ the investment proposals were reasonable] ; (on the other hand) heⓢ had reached ⓥ no final decision ⓞ ⟨on them⟩.

【訳】Achmed氏はその投資の提案を無理のないものだと思ったが、他方では彼は最終決定に至っていなかった。

- ☐ furthermore　副さらに
- ☐ in case　接……するといけないから
- ☐ in order that　接……する目的で
- ☐ reasonable　形理にかなった

18. 正解 (D)

【解説】an address about ~（~に関する演説）から考えて、空所には about（~について）を入れ「演説は~に関するものになるだろう」という意味にするのが適当。

構造 The keynote address ⓢ ⟨at the conference⟩ will be ⓥ (about the impact) ⟨of online advertisements⟩⟨in global markets⟩.

【訳】会議の基調演説は、世界市場でのオンライン広告の影響に関するものになるだろう。

- ☐ of　前~の
- ☐ to　前~の方へ
- ☐ around　前~の周囲に
- ☐ keynote address　名基調演説

19. 正解 (B)

【解説】空所の後ろは「名詞+修飾節」の形なので、空所には前置詞に相当する語句が入る。「出席者が持っているかもしれない（どんな質問であれ）最後の質問は別にして」と考えて、空所には apart from（~はさておき）を入れる。

構造 Mr. Gupta ⓢ said ⓥ [ⓞ he was ready to dismiss the conferees, (apart from any last questions ⟨participants might have had⟩)].

【訳】会議はそろそろ終わる用意ができているけれど、最後に参加者からどんな質問でも受け付けます、とGupta氏は言った。

- ☐ once　接いったん……すると
- ☐ whereupon　副その上
- ☐ dismiss　動解散させる
- ☐ conferee　名会議出席者
- ☐ participant　名参加者

20. 正解 (C)

【解説】空所の後ろが完全な文の形になっていることと、「労働者を追加雇用する」という内容から考えて、assuming that（……と仮定して）を入れる。

構造 (According to media reports), Kuanda Inc. ⓢ will hire ⓥ an additional 550 workers ⓞ, (assuming [that product demand continues [to increase (at present rates)]]).

【訳】マスコミの報道によれば、Kuanda社は製品需要が現在の割合で増加し続けると見込んで、550人の労働者を追加雇用するだろう。

- ☐ according to ~　熟~によると
- ☐ demand　名需要；必要性

意味や用法が適した接続詞・前置詞・論理マーカーの選択

21. Assembly line production levels were greatly increased, ------- the equipment there could be operated safely.

(A) insofar as
(B) or else
(C) if ever
(D) only if

22. Sales of cereal bars are forecast to rise by 4% this quarter ------- their prices can remain stable during that same period.

(A) only if
(B) during
(C) as such
(D) but also

23. Ms. Isabel Kwak is one of the best-known entrepreneurs in Malaysia, ------- she is also one of the most successful.

(A) ever since
(B) once
(C) with regard to
(D) seeing that

24. Harrigan Department Store will be closed until May 30 ------- a planned building expansion.

(A) due to
(B) as outlined
(C) because
(D) near to

21. 正解　(A)

【解説】まぎらわしい接続詞が並んでいるが、insofar as（.....する範囲で ; .....する限り）を入れるのが意味的に最も自然。

構造 Assembly line production levels ⓢ were (greatly) increased ⓥ, (insofar as the equipment (there) could be operated (safely)).

【訳】組み立てラインの生産水準は、設備が安全に操作できる範囲で大幅に引き上げられた。

- □ or else　　接 さもないと
- □ if ever　　接 もし.....だとしても
- □ only if　　接 .....の場合に限り
- □ greatly　　副 非常に
- □ operate　　動 操作する
- □ safely　　副 安全に

22. 正解　(A)

【解説】空所の後ろが完全な文の形なので、空所には接続詞が入る。but also は前の not only と結合して「～だけでなく…も」なので、ここでは only if（.....の場合に限り）を入れるのが適当。

構造 Sales ⓢ 〈of cereal bars〉 are forecast ⓥ to rise (by 4%) (this quarter) (only if their prices can remain stable during that same period).

【訳】シリアルバーの今四半期の売り上げは、同期間中に価格が維持されていれば、4％の上昇が見込まれる。

- □ during　　前 ～の間中
- □ as such　　熟 そういうものとして
- □ forecast　　動 予想する
- □ stable　　形 安定した

23. 正解　(D)

【解説】空所の後ろの形から考えて空所には接続詞が入るが、意味から考えて seeing that（.....にかんがみて ; .....であるから）を入れるのが適当。

構造 Ms. Isabel Kwak ⓢ is ⓥ one ⓒ 〈of the best-known entrepreneurs〉〈in Malaysia〉〉, (seeing that she is also one 〈of the most successful〉).

【訳】Isabel Kwak 氏は、最も成功した人物の一人であることからも、マレーシアで最も有名な起業家の一人だ。

- □ ever since　　接 それ以来ずっと
- □ once　　接 いったん.....すると
- □ with regard to ～　　熟 ～に関しては
- □ best-known　　形 最もよく知られた
- □ entrepreneur　　名 起業家

24. 正解　(A)

【解説】空所の後ろは名詞句なので、空所には前置詞に相当する語句が入る。意味から考えて、due to ～（～のために）が適当。because は接続詞だから使えない。

構造 Harrigan Department Store ⓢ will be closed ⓥ (until May 30) (due to a planned building expansion).

【訳】Harrigan デパートは、増築を予定しているため5月30日まで休業いたします。

- □ because　　接 .....だから

25. Hilstrom Financial Group reported operational improvements in many areas ------- its corporate and investment banking division.
 (A) in line to
 (B) otherwise
 (C) apart from
 (D) as arranged

26. Several employees expressed their interest in the department head vacancy ------- it became known to them.
 (A) concerning
 (B) as for
 (C) beyond which
 (D) the instant

27. All goods leaving the manufacturer's main distribution center in New Delhi are electronically tagged before being loaded ------- trucks.
 (A) from
 (B) over
 (C) onto
 (D) down

28. The production manager made some pleasant remarks ------- the decreasing absenteeism among staff.
 (A) on the grounds that
 (B) so that
 (C) although
 (D) concerning

25. 正解 (C)

【解説】空所の後ろは名詞句なので、空所には前置詞に相当する語句が入る。意味から考えて、apart from ~(~は別にして)が適当。as arranged(予定どおりに)は副詞句だから使えない。

構造 Hilstrom Financial Group ⓢ reported ⓥ |operational improvements| ⓞ 〈in many areas〉 (apart from its corporate and investment banking division).

【訳】Hilstrom Financial Groupは、法人・投資銀行業務の部門は除いて、多くの分野で業務が改善したことを公表した。

□ operational improvement 名業務改善

26. 正解 (D)

【解説】空所の後ろが完全な文の形であることを考慮して、空所にはas soon asと同じ意味を表すthe instant (.....するとすぐに)を入れるのが適当。

構造 Several employees ⓢ expressed ⓥ |their interest| ⓞ 〈in the department head vacancy〉 (the instant it became known (to them)).

【訳】部長のポストが空いたことが知れ渡るとすぐに、数人の社員が関心を示した。

□ concerning 前~に関して　　□ as for ~ 熟~について言えば
□ express 動表現する　　　　□ interest 名関心

27. 正解 (C)

【解説】load A onto Bで「AをBに積む」の意味を表すので、空所にはonto (~の上に)が入る。fromやoverは使わない。

構造 |All goods| ⓢ 〈leaving |the manufacturer's main distribution center| 〈in New Delhi〉〉 are (electronically) tagged ⓥ (before being loaded (onto trucks)).

【訳】ニューデリーにあるそのメーカーの本部配送センターを出るすべての製品は、トラックに積み込まれる前に電子タグがつけられる。

□ from 前~から　　　　　□ over 前~の上方に　　□ down 前~の下へ
□ manufacturer 名製造業者　□ electronically 副電子装置で　□ tag 動荷札を付ける

28. 正解 (D)

【解説】空所の後ろが完成した文の形ではなく名詞句なので、空所には前置詞の働きをするconcerning (~に関して)が入る。

構造 The production manager ⓢ made ⓥ some pleasant remarks ⓞ (concerning |the decreasing absenteeism| 〈among staff〉).

【訳】職員の常習的欠勤が減ったことに関して、生産部長は愛想の良い発言をした。

□ on the grounds that 熟.....という理由で　□ so that 熟.....するために　□ although 接.....だけれども
□ pleasant 形愛想のいい　　　　　　　　□ remark 名意見　　　　　　　□ absenteeism 名常習的欠勤

29. Ms. Bhatia was asked to manage customer exchanges and refunds, ------- supervising the store's fitting rooms.
   (A) considering that
   (B) on the grounds that
   (C) in addition to
   (D) to the extent

30. The Trison Co. CEO announced that ------- the recent economic downturn, the company had experienced a record increase in profits.
   (A) in turn
   (B) regardless of
   (C) such as
   (D) for the sake of

31. Hotel guests who lose their room key must pay a £10 charge ------- they are issued a replacement.
   (A) before
   (B) for
   (C) against
   (D) over

32. The sales assistant told Ms. Haufmann that her purchased items could be returned within 30 days, ------- they were undamaged.
   (A) provided that
   (B) according to
   (C) due to
   (D) in case of

29. 正解 (C)

【解説】空所の後ろは完全な文の形ではなくsupervising（監督すること）で始まる名詞句なので、空所には前置詞のin addition to ～（～に加えて）が入る。

構造 Ms. Bhatia (s) was asked (v) to manage customer exchanges and refunds, (in addition to [supervising the store's fitting rooms]).

【訳】Bhatia氏は、店の試着室の管理に加えて、顧客への商品交換と返金の管理も頼まれた。

□considering that	(接)…… であるわりには	□on the grounds that	(接)…… という理由で
□exchange	(名)交換	□refund	(名)払い戻し
□supervise	(動)管理する	□fitting room	(名)試着室

30. 正解 (B)

【解説】economic downturn（景気の低迷）とincrease in profits（増益）とは相反する内容だから、空所にはregardless of ～（～に関係なく；～にかかわらず）を入れる。

構造 The Trison Co. CEO (s) announced (v) [(o) that (regardless of the recent economic downturn), the company had experienced a record increase ⟨in profits⟩].

【訳】Trison社のCEOは、最近の不況にもかかわらず同社は記録的な増益を達成したと発表した。

| □in turn | (熟)順番に | □such as | (熟)例えば～など | □for the sake of ～ | (熟)～ために |
| □announce | (動)発表する | □economic downturn | (名)景気の低迷 | □increase in profits | (名)増益 |

31. 正解 (A)

【解説】空所の後ろが完全な文の形になっているので、空所には前置詞ではなく接続詞が入る。選択肢のうち接続詞として使えるのはbefore（…… する前に）だけなので、これを入れる。

構造 Hotel guests (s) ⟨who lose their room key⟩ must pay (v) a £10 charge (o), (before they are issued a replacement).

【訳】部屋の鍵をなくした宿泊客は、代わりの鍵を発行してもらうのに10ポンドの料金を支払わねばならない。

| □for | (前)～のために | □against | (前)～に反対して | □over | (前)～の上に |
| □charge | (名)手数料 | □issue | (動)発行する | □replacement | (名)代用品 |

32. 正解 (A)

【解説】空所の後ろが完全な文の形であることから考えて、接続詞の働きをするprovided that（…… という条件で；もし……なら）を入れる。

構造 The sales assistant (s) told (v) Ms. Haufmann (o) [(o) that her purchased items could be returned (within 30 days), (provided that they were undamaged)].

【訳】購入した品に損傷がなければ30日以内に返品できます、と販売員はHaufmann氏に言った。

| □according to ～ | (熟)～によれば | □due to ～ | (熟)～のため | □in case of ～ | (熟)～の場合には |
| □purchased | (形)購入された | □undamaged | (形)損害を受けていない |

意味や用法が適した接続詞・前置詞・論理マーカーの選択

33. The customer service representative promised to urgently look ------- Ms. Gashi's missing shipment problem.
(A) as
(B) into
(C) above
(D) out

34. Oduba's Co.'s strategy, ------- its slow but growing brand recognition, focused on greater marketing efforts.
(A) once
(B) moreover
(C) however
(D) regarding

35. Customers wishing to use the fitting rooms located ------- the main registers should contact a store assistant.
(A) since
(B) until
(C) past
(D) like

36. Mr. Solanga's supervisor asked him to continue at his job ------ the company could find a suitable replacement for him.
(A) except
(B) yet
(C) until
(D) whereas

33. 正解 (B)

【解説】lookと結びついて他動詞の働きをするイディオムを作るのは、選択肢中ではintoのみ。look into ～で「～を調査する」の意味を表す。

構造 The customer service representative ⓢ promised ⓥ [ⓞ to (urgently) look into Ms. Gashi's missing shipment problem].

【訳】顧客サービス部の担当者は、Gashi氏の紛失した荷物の問題を緊急に調査すると約束した。

- □ promise ⑩約束する　　□ urgently ⑳緊急に　　□ missing ㊗紛失している

34. 正解 (D)

【解説】カンマではさまれた部分が修飾語（副詞）の働きをする形。空所の後ろが名詞句なので、前置詞に近い働きをするregarding（～を考慮して；～に関して）を入れる。

構造 Oduba's Co.'s strategy, ⓢ (regarding its slow but growing brand recognition), focused ⓥ (on greater marketing efforts).

【訳】Oduba's社の戦略は、徐々にではあるが浸透しつつあるブランド認知を考慮して、宣伝広告にさらに重点的に努力を傾けた。

- □ once ㊗いったん.....すると　　□ moreover ⑳その上　　□ however ⑳けれども
- □ strategy ㊅戦略　　□ recognition ㊅認知　　□ effort ㊅努力

35. 正解 (C)

【解説】be located（位置する）の後ろに置く前置詞としては、past（～を過ぎたところに；～の先に）が適当。

構造 Customers ⓢ ⟨wishing to use the fitting rooms ⟨located past the main registers⟩⟩ should contact ⓥ a store assistant ⓞ.

【訳】中央レジの先にある試着室をご利用になりたいお客様は、店員にご連絡ください。

- □ since ㊠～以来　　□ until ㊠～までずっと　　□ like ㊠～に似た
- □ wish to V ㊗Vしたいと思う　　□ located ㊗位置している

36. 正解 (C)

【解説】空所には接続詞が入る。「会社が彼の後任を見つける（　　）」の空所に入る適当な接続詞はuntil（.....するまで）。

構造 Mr. Solanga's supervisor ⓢ asked ⓥ him ⓞ to continue (at his job) (until the company could find a suitable replacement ⟨for him⟩).

【訳】Solanga氏の上司は、会社が彼の適当な後任者を見つけられるまで仕事を続けてほしいと彼に頼んだ。

- □ except ㊠～を除いて　　□ yet ⑳しかし　　□ whereas ㊗....だが一方
- □ suitable ㊗適した　　□ replacement ㊅交替者

意味や用法が適した接続詞・前置詞・論理マーカーの選択

37. Mr. Samaweera signs ------- on any expense claims from his sales team at the end of each month.
    (A) through
    (B) after
    (C) off
    (D) by

    Ⓐ Ⓑ Ⓒ Ⓓ

38. The CEO thanked Mr. Ndana ------- the entire board for all his hard work and wished him a happy retirement.
    (A) beyond which
    (B) on behalf of
    (C) in case of
    (D) as applied to

    Ⓐ Ⓑ Ⓒ Ⓓ

39. Mr. Akram arrived in Boston ------- schedule so he could acquaint himself with all materials relevant to the upcoming conference.
    (A) ahead of
    (B) in addition to
    (C) until which
    (D) up to

    Ⓐ Ⓑ Ⓒ Ⓓ

40. More Johannesburg residents this year are making major landscaping improvements ------- adding new lawn grass, flowers, and bushes.
    (A) across
    (B) onto
    (C) by
    (D) to

    Ⓐ Ⓑ Ⓒ Ⓓ

37. 正解 (C)

【解説】sign（署名する）と結びついてイディオムを作るのはoff。sign off on ～で「～を承認する」の意味を表す。

構造 Mr. Samaweera ⓢ signs off ⓥ (on any expense claims ⟨from his sales team⟩) (at the end of each month).

【訳】Samaweera氏は、毎月末に営業チームから出てきた経費の請求は何でも承認する。

□ claim 图請求

38. 正解 (B)

【解説】thank A for B で「AにBのことで感謝する」の意味を表すので、Mr. Ndanaとforとの間に修飾語句が挿入された形と解釈する。前後の文脈から考えて、空所にはon behalf of ～（～を代表して）を入れる。

構造 The CEO ⓢ thanked ⓥ1 Mr. Ndana ⓞ1 (on behalf of the entire board) (for all his hard work) and wished ⓥ2 him ⓞ1 a happy retirement ⓞ2.

【訳】CEOは全役員を代表してNdana氏の労苦に感謝し、円満な退職を祈った。

□ board 图役員（会）　　　□ wish 動祈る　　　□ retirement 图退職

39. 正解 (A)

【解説】空所の後ろのscheduleと結びついて意味をなすのはahead of ～（～の先に）。ahead of scheduleで「予定より早く」の意味。反意表現はbehind schedule（予定より遅れて）。

構造 Mr. Akram ⓢ arrived ⓥ (in Boston) (ahead of schedule) (so he could acquaint himself (with all materials ⟨relevant to the upcoming conference⟩)).

【訳】Akram氏は来るべき会議に関連するすべての資料を熟知しておくことができるよう、予定より早くボストンに到着した。

□ in addition to ～ 熟～に加えて　　　□ up to ～ 熟～まで
□ acquaint A with B 熟AにBを熟知させる　　　□ relevant to ～ 熟～と関係があって　　　□ upcoming 形今度の

40. 正解 (C)

【解説】空所の前のmake ... improvements（改良する）と後ろのadding（加えること）から考えて、空所にはby（～によって）を入れて「加えることによって改良する」とするのが適当。

構造 More Johannesburg residents ⓢ (this year) are making ⓥ major landscaping improvements ⓞ (by adding new lawn grass, flowers, and bushes).

【訳】ヨハネスブルグでは今年、新しく芝生や花や低木を植えることによって庭の景観を大幅に改良する住人が増えている。

□ across 前～を横切って　　　□ onto 前～の上へ　　　□ to 前～の方へ
□ landscaping 图造園　　　□ improvement 图改良　　　□ lawn grass 图芝
□ bush 图低木

意味や用法が適した接続詞・前置詞・論理マーカーの選択

Lesson 8

Part6 対策
設問の直前・直後、プラスとマイナスの視点を

◆まずは直前と直後を確認！◆

　TOEICのPart 6は、電子メールなどの長文の中に空所補充問題がありますが、**出題されるポイント自体は、パート5と大きな差はありません**。ただし、前後の文の流れを把握した上で、考えなければならない問題も出てくるので、気をつけなければなりません。

　解答の手順としては、まず**空所の直前、直後の情報だけで問題が解けるかどうか**を確認しましょう。単なる語彙の選択の問題などであれば、その場で解答し、すぐに次の設問に進むとよいでしょう。

　一方、論理マーカーのhoweverやthereforeなどの選択問題など、前後の文脈をある程度大きくつかまなければ解答できない問題の場合は、前後数行を読み、文脈を探った上で解答しましょう。

　このように、Part 6に関しては、**英文すべてを細部まで読む必要はありません**。

◆プラスとマイナスの視点を持つ◆

　文章の中に空所補充が設けられた設問を解く際には、**前後から空所に入るもののカテゴリーを絞り込む習慣を身につける**ことが大事です。どのような品詞が入るのか、物なのか人なのか、などを頭の中で絞り込んでいきます。

　特に重要なのが、**大小**、**善悪**、**長短**、のように**プラスとマイナス**の二極に別れるものです。

　例えば、顧客の製品に対する反応を述べている空所の選択肢にsatisfied（満足している→プラス）、disappointed（がっかりしている→マイナス）のような単語が並べられていたとします。その場合、前後の文脈から、顧客が「喜んでいる→プラス」「喜んでいない→マイナス」を割り出せば、どちらが正解かがわかるわけです。

◆論理マーカーの絞り込み◆

論理マーカーは以下の４つのカテゴリーに分類して考えます。

1	順接	therefore as a result in conclusion consequently	それゆえに その結果 結論として その結果
2	逆接	however on the other hand yet nevertheless	しかしながら その一方で しかし それでもなお
3	追加	besides in addition moreover furthermore	それに加えて それに加えて さらに さらに
4	同格(具体化) 同格(要約) 同格(換言)	for example such as 〜 briefly in short in other words	たとえば 〜のような 手短に言えば 要するに 別の言い方では

　前後の意味的流れから、上記のどのパターンで前後の論理がつながっているのかを見抜きます。そしてそれに従って選択肢を選んで行けばよいわけです。これらを選ぶ問題では、ある程度大きく空所の前後を読む必要があります。

EXERCISES

空所補充 文章を完全な形にするために、必要な語句を1つだけ選んでください。

Questions 1-3 refer to the following advertisement.

INTERNATIONAL BUSINESS SCHOOL OF TOKYO (IBST)

With convenient class locations in downtown Tokyo, as well as online learning, IBST makes quality business education highly accessible for working students. We can help you reach your goal in a variety of business fields ------- from finance to marketing.

    1. (A) ranges
       (B) ranged
       (C) ranging
       (D) range

About IBST

With our extensive network around the Tokyo metropolitan area, you can attend classes at one of our 46 convenient locations, or sign up for our online classes so you can continue your education while accommodating your busy schedule. You'll receive a real-world business education with real -------, regardless of where or how you attend class.

    2. (A) valuable
       (B) value
       (C) valued
       (D) invaluable

Quality Business Education. Highly Accessible.
Acquire the knowledge and skills that are in high demand.
Receive personal attention in small, interactive classes.
Learn from instructors who have ------- experience in the fields they teach.

    3. (A) coherent
       (B) substantial
       (C) predictable
       (D) available

Attend class at times and places that fit your schedule.

For further information please contact us at 0120-100-1111

Part 6 と同じ形式の問題です。小問 3 題からなる 4 つの文章を、それぞれ 1 分で解き進めてください。

---

1. 正解 (C)
【解説】range from A to B は「範囲が A から B に及ぶ」という意味の重要表現。ここでは、分詞として形容詞的に、直前の business fields という名詞句を修飾している。

2. 正解 (B)
【解説】with という前置詞の目的語となる部分なので名詞の value（価値）が適切である。他の選択肢は形容詞の働きをするものなので、答えにはならない。valuable は「価値がある」、valued は「評価された」、invaluable は「貴重な」という意味。

3. 正解 (B)
【解説】experience という名詞を修飾する形容詞として、意味的に最も適切なものを選ぶ。substantial（実質的な；十分な）が最も文意に合っている。coherent は「首尾一貫した」、predictable は「予測可能な」、available は「入手可能な」という意味。

文構造

INTERNATIONAL BUSINESS SCHOOL OF TOKYO (IBST)

(With convenient class locations ⟨in downtown Tokyo⟩), (as well as online learning), IBST makes quality business education (highly) accessible (for working students). We can help you reach your goal (in a variety of business fields ⟨ranging from finance to marketing⟩).

About IBST

(With our extensive network ⟨around the Tokyo metropolitan area⟩), you can attend classes (at one ⟨of our 46 convenient locations⟩), or sign up (for our online classes) (so you can continue your education (while accommodating your busy schedule)). You 'll receive a real-world business education ⟨with real value⟩, (regardless of [where or how you attend class]).

Quality Business Education. Highly Accessible.
Acquire the knowledge and skills ⟨that are in high demand⟩.
Receive personal attention (in small, interactive classes).
Learn (from instructors ⟨who have substantial experience ⟨in the fields ⟨they teach⟩⟩⟩).
Attend class (at times and places ⟨that fit your schedule⟩).

(For further information) (please) contact us (at 0120-100-1111)

文章の訳

INTERNATIONAL BUSINESS SCHOOL OF TOKYO (IBST)

　東京都心部に位置する便利な教室とオンライン学習により、IBST は、高品位なビジネス教育を、働きながら学ぶみなさまにとって十分に利用可能なものとします。金融からマーケティングまで、ビジネスのさまざまな分野において、みなさまの目標達成のお手伝いをいたします。

IBST とは

　東京首都圏周辺での充実したネットワークにより、立地条件に恵まれた 46 の教室のひとつで学習していただくこともできますし、多忙なスケジュールをこなしつつ学習を継続するためオンライン教室にサインアップしていただくこともできます。受講の場所や手段を問わず、真に価値のある実社会でのビジネス教育があなたのものとなります。

　高品質のビジネス教育。学習に大変便利。
　必要性の高い知識と技能の獲得。
　小規模な双方向学習による十分な個別配慮。
　指導分野での豊かな経験を持つ講師陣。
　個人の都合に合わせた時間と場所での受講。

　お問い合わせは、0120-100-1111 まで、お電話で。

◆ ボキャブラリー ◆

☐ convenient	形便利な；立地条件に恵まれた	☐ accommodate	動こなす；対応する
☐ downtown	名都心部	☐ busy schedule	名多忙なスケジュール
☐ online learning	名オンライン学習	☐ real-world	形実社会の
☐ quality	形高品位な	☐ valuable	形価値がある
☐ business education	名ビジネス教育	☐ value	名価値
☐ accessible	形利用可能な	☐ valued	形評価された
☐ working student	名働きながら学ぶ人	☐ invaluable	形貴重な
☐ a variety of ~	熟さまざまな～	☐ regardless of ~	熟～を問わず
☐ business field	名ビジネス分野	☐ acquire	動獲得する
☐ range from A to B	熟 A から B までの範囲に及ぶ	☐ personal attention	名個別配慮
☐ finance	名金融	☐ interactive	形双方向の
☐ extensive	形広範囲にわたる	☐ coherent	形首尾一貫した
☐ the Tokyo metropolitan area	名東京首都圏	☐ substantial	形十分な
		☐ predictable	形予測可能な
☐ sign up for ~	熟～に申し込む	☐ available	形入手できる
☐ online class	名オンライン教室		

Questions 4-6 refer to the following e-mail.

To: Sarah Green<sarah@mmk.com>
From: Mark Goldwire<mark-g@WinGold.com>
Sent: Tuesday, September 19
Subject: Overdue payment

Dear Ms. Green,

This letter is in regards to your overdue payment. We have sent you letters about the overdue payment several times this month, but as of yet we have not ------- any payment.

4. (A) receive
(B) receiving
(C) receives
(D) received

If there is any reason you are unable to make the payment, please let us know -------.

5. (A) immediately
(B) forcibly
(C) increasingly
(D) continuously

We may be able to reschedule your payment plan. If we do not receive a reply by the end of this month, we will have no choice but to initiate legal procedures.

We would like to continue to offer our best ------- to you, and we value and appreciate your business.

6. (A) service
(B) expectation
(C) acceptance
(D) influence

Attached is another copy of the invoice.

Mark Goldwire
Payment Service
001- 344 – 5461 Ext. 988

4. 正解 **(D)**
【解説】空所の直前の have は現在完了形を作るための助動詞の have と考えられるので、過去分詞形の received が正解となる。

5. 正解 **(A)**
【解説】文の意味に最も合っている、immediately（即座に）という副詞が正解。forcibly は「強制的に」、increasingly は「ますます」、continuously は「継続的に」という意味。

6. 正解 **(A)**
【解説】offer という他動詞の目的語として、文の意味に最も合っている service（業務；サービス）という名詞が正解。expectation は「期待」、acceptance は「受諾」、influence は「影響」という意味。

文構造

To: Sarah Green<sarah@mmk.com>

From: Mark Goldwire<mark-g@WinGold.com>

Sent: Tuesday, September 19

Subject: Overdue payment

Dear Ms. Green,

This letter (S) is (V) in regards to your overdue payment (O). We (S) have sent (V) you (O) letters (O) ⟨about the overdue payment⟩ (several times) (this month), but (as of yet) we (S) have not received (V) any payment (O).

(If there is any reason ⟨you are unable to make the payment⟩), (please) let (V) us (O) know (immediately). We (S) may be (V) able (C) to reschedule your payment plan. (If we do not receive a reply (by the end ⟨of this month⟩)), we (S) will have (V) no choice (O) ⟨but to initiate legal procedures⟩.

We (S) would like (V) [(O) to continue [to offer our best service (to you)]], and we (S) value and appreciate (V) your business (O).

Attached (C) is (V) another copy (S) ⟨of the invoice⟩.

Mark Goldwire

Payment Service

001- 344 – 5461 Ext. 988

文章の訳

宛先：Sarah Green<sarah@mmk.com>
送信者：Mark Goldwire<mark-g@WinGold.com>
日付：9月19日（火）
件名：支払延滞

Ms. Green 様

本件は、お客様の支払延滞についてのお知らせです。今月、数回にわたり、当社からお客様への支払延滞のご連絡を差し上げましたが、現在のところ、お支払をいただいておりません。

もしお支払いただけない事情がおありでしたら、速やかに当社にご連絡ください。お客様の支払計画を変更させていただくことができるかもしれません。もし、今月末までにお返事をいただけない場合、当社では法的手続きの開始を余儀なくされます。

当社では、お客様へ最高のサービス提供を継続することを願いつつ、御社の事業に心より感謝の念を表します。

納品伝票の写しを添付いたします。

Mark Goldwire
支払業務
001-344-5461 内線 988

◆ ボキャブラリー ◆

☐ overdue	形 期日を過ぎた	☐ have no choice but to V	熟 余儀なくVする
☐ several times	名 数回		
☐ as of yet	熟 まだ現在のところ	☐ initiate	動 開始する
☐ make payment	熟 支払いをする	☐ legal procedure	名 法的手続き
☐ immediately	副 即座に	☐ expectation	名 期待
☐ forcibly	副 強制的に	☐ acceptance	名 受諾
☐ increasingly	副 ますます	☐ influence	名 影響
☐ continuously	副 継続的に	☐ appreciate	動 感謝する
☐ reschedule	動 変更する	☐ attach	動 添付する
☐ payment plan	名 支払計画	☐ invoice	名 納品伝票
☐ reply	名 返事		

Questions 7-9 refer to the following e-mail.

To: Mary Goldwin<mary-G@servingworld.com>
From: Adam Jones<adamjones@InfoSoftTech.com>
Sent: Tuesday, May 3
Subject: Information requested

Thank you for your interest in our service. ------- , I am afraid that we will not be

      7. (A) Therefore
          (B) However
          (C) Besides
          (D) Briefly

able to supply you with the information you requested.

We have a strict policy of not disclosing any of our data processing procedures. ------- this sort of information would jeopardize our long-term relationships with

8. (A) Providing
   (B) Provided
   (C) Provides
   (D) Provision

our network partners.

What we can tell you is that our system is based on a Tri-X database by INTERSOFT, and the customer list ------- and their privacy shoud be safe in any circumstances.

      9. (A) classified
          (B) is classified
          (C) classifying
          (D) be classified

Adam Jones
Database Center
001- 234-7458 Ext. 232

7. 正解　(B)
【解説】空所の前の文ではメールの差出人に対して礼を述べている。つまりプラスの内容。一方、後ろの文では期待に添えないことが述べられている。つまりマイナスの内容。このように、前後の内容が反対の方向性の場合に使うのは、however（しかしながら）という逆接の接続副詞。therefore は「それゆえに」、besides は「それに加えて」、briefly は「要するに；手短に言えば」という意味。

8. 正解　(A)
【解説】空所は would jeopardize を述部とする、文全体の主語の部分にある。そして主語には名詞が置かれるため、名詞の働きをするものを選ぶ。なお、名詞ではあるが provision（用意）だと直後の名詞とつながらないため、目的語を続けることができる providing という動名詞が正解となる。

9. 正解　(B)
【解説】classified は「極秘の；分類された」という意味の形容詞。主語の customer list にこれを続けるためには、be 動詞が必要となる。主語に合わせて is が使われているものが正解。もともとの classify という動詞は「分類する」という意味。

文構造

To: Mary Goldwin<mary-G@servingworld.com>

From: Adam Jones<adamjones@InfoSoftTech.com>

Sent: Tuesday, May 3

Subject: Information requested

Thank(v) you(c) (for |your interest| ⟨in our service⟩). (However), I(s) am(v) afraid(c) [that we will not be able to supply you (with | the information | ⟨you requested⟩)].

We(s) have(v) |a strict policy|(c) ⟨of [not disclosing | any | ⟨of our data processing procedures⟩]⟩. [(s)Providing this sort of information] would jeopardize(v) |our long-term relationships|(c) ⟨with our network partners⟩.

[(s)What we can tell you] is(v) [(c)that our system is based on |a Tri-X database| ⟨by INTERSOFT⟩], and the customer list(s) is classified(v), and their privacy(s) should be(v) safe(c) (in any circumstances)].

Adam Jones
Database Center
001- 234-7458 Ext. 232

文章の訳

宛先：Mary Goldwin<mary-G@servingworld.com>
送信者：Adam Jones<adamjones@InfoSoftTech.com>
日付：5月3日（火）
件名：ご依頼の情報について

当社のサービスにご関心をお寄せいただき、ありがとうございます。しかしながら、申し訳ございませんが、ご依頼の情報は提供できません。

当社では、あらゆるデータ処理手順に関しては非公開とする厳格な方針を採用しております。こうした情報の提供は、当社のネットワーク・パートナーとの長期的関係を危険にさらしかねません。

お客様にお伝えできることとしては、当社のシステムがINTERSOFT社のTri-Xデータベースを基盤としており、顧客リストは極秘扱いとして、顧客のプライバシーはいかなる場合でも安全に管理いたしております。

Adam Jones
データベースセンター
001- 234-7458 内線 232

◆ ボキャブラリー ◆

- therefore　副それゆえに
- however　副しかしながら
- besides　副それに加えて
- briefly　副要するに
- request　動依頼する
- afraid　形申し訳なく思う
- supply　動提供する
- strict　形厳格な
- disclose　動公開する
- processing　名処理
- provision　名用意
- jeopardize　動危険にさらす
- relationship　名関係
- customer list　名顧客リスト
- classified　形極秘の；分類された
- safe　形安全な
- circumstances　名状況

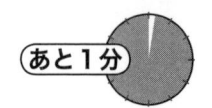

Questions 10-12 refer to the following advertisement.

HELP WANTED

USE YOUR KNOWLEDGE FOR TRAVEL ADVERTISEMENT

MAX TOUR VALUE ASIA is seeking applicants for the position of PR Officer in our Beijing office. Previous PR experience, ------ knowledge of various Asian

    10. (A) as well as
        (B) due to
        (C) on behalf of
        (D) according to

tourist spots, such as Bali and Phuket, is highly desirable. Ability to speak fluently and write clearly in English and Chinese is essential. Knowledge of other Asian languages would be a great advantage.

Candidates should e-mail an application and resume in English and Chinese to Chun@j-research.cn by Nov. 30. Only ------- candidates will be contacted by e-mail.

    11. (A) successive
        (B) successful
        (C) succeeded
        (D) success

We do not accept telephone inquiries.

MAX TOUR VALUE ASIA has operated at several locations in China, Korea and Japan for over fifteen years, --------- to the needs of the travelers who seek an

    12. (A) acquiring
        (B) demanding
        (C) dropping
        (D) catering

experience different from those they can gain through common group tours.

10. 正解　**(A)**
【解説】空所の直前には「経験」、直後には「知識」という、仕事で求められる要素が並べられている。これらを結ぶことができるのは、A as well as B（B と同様にAも）のみ。due to 〜は「〜のために」、on behalf of 〜は「〜の代わりに」、according to 〜は「〜によれば」という意味。

11. 正解　**(B)**
【解説】直後に candidates という名詞があることから、空所には形容詞が入ると考えられる。選択肢の中で文の意味に合っているのは、successful（成功した）。successive は「連続した」という意味の形容詞で意味が合わない。success は「成功」という意味の名詞。

12. 正解　**(D)**
【解説】cater という動詞は to という前置詞と結びつき、cater to 〜という形で「〜（要望）に応ずる」という意味になる。acquire は「獲得する」、demand は「要求する」、drop は「落とす」という意味なので、文の意味に合わない。

HELP WANTED

USE YOUR KNOWLEDGE (FOR TRAVEL ADVERTISEMENT)

MAX TOUR VALUE ASIA is seeking applicants 〈for the position 〈of PR Officer 〈in our Beijing office〉〉〉. Previous PR experience, as well as knowledge 〈of various Asian tourist spots, 〈such as Bali and Phuket〉〉, is (highly) desirable. Ability 〈to speak (fluently) and write (clearly) (in English and Chinese)〉 is essential. Knowledge 〈of other Asian languages〉 would be a great advantage.

Candidates should e-mail an application and resume 〈in English and Chinese〉 (to Chun@j-research.cn) (by Nov. 30). Only successful candidates will be contacted (by e-mail). We do not accept telephone inquiries.

MAX TOUR VALUE ASIA has operated (at several locations 〈in China, Korea and Japan〉) (for over fifteen years), (catering to the needs 〈of the travelers 〈who seek an experience 〈different (from those 〈they can gain (through common group tours)〉〉〉〉〉).

文章の訳

人材募集

あなたの知識を旅行広告に活かしましょう

　MAX TOUR VALUE ASIA 社では、当社北京事務所での広報担当職への応募者を募集中。これまでの広報経験、バリ、プーケットなど、アジア各地の観光地の知識は大歓迎。英語および中国語の流暢な会話力と確かな文章力は必須。他のアジア言語の知識があれば大いに優遇。

　応募者は、11月30日までに英語および中国語の応募申込書および経歴書を Chun@j-research.cn まで E メールで送付。選考通過者のみ E メールでご連絡いたします。電話での問い合わせは不可。

　MAX TOUR VALUE ASIA 社は、中国、韓国、日本の拠点で、15年以上にわたり事業展開し、一般のグループツアーで得られるものとは異なる経験を求める旅行者のご要望にお応えしてまいりました。

◆ ボキャブラリー ◆

□ help wanted	熟 人材募集	□ essential	形 不可欠な
□ knowledge	名 知識	□ candidate	名 応募者
□ seek	動 求める	□ application	名 申込書
□ applicant	名 応募者	□ resume	名 経歴書
□ A as well as B	熟 B と同様に A も	□ successive	形 連続した
□ due to ～	熟 ～のために	□ successful	形 成功した
□ on behalf of ～	熟 ～の代わりに	□ success	名 成功
□ according to ～	熟 ～によれば	□ inquiry	名 問い合わせ
□ tourist spot	名 観光地	□ acquire	動 獲得する
□ desirable	形 望ましい	□ demand	動 要求する
□ fluently	副 流暢に	□ drop	動 落とす
□ clearly	副 明らかに	□ cater to ～	熟 ～に応ずる

◆重要接尾辞一覧◆

　TOEIC テストでは、選択肢の中に、語幹は同じであっても接尾辞が異なる単語が並べられることがあります。そのような場合には接尾辞の知識が役に立ちます。

名詞を作る接尾辞

□ -ee	～される人	employ（雇用する）	→ employee（雇用される人→従業員）
□ -ion	～すること	act（行動する）	→ action（行動）
□ -ment	～すること	achieve（獲得する）	→ achievement（業績）
□ -ant	～する人	assist（助ける）	→ assistant（助手）
□ -er[or]	～する人	employ（雇う）	→ employer（雇用者）
□ -ist	～する人	essay（エッセイ）	→ essayist（エッセイスト）
□ -dom	～であること	free（自由な）	→ freedom（自由）
□ -ness	～であること	fair（公正な）	→ fairness（公正）
□ -ship	～であること	friend（友人）	→ friendship（友情）
□ -logy	～学	zoo（動物園）	→ zoology（動物学）
□ -ics	～学	economy（経済）	→ economics（経済学）
□ -ism	～主義	capital（資本）	→ capitalism（資本主義）

形容詞を作る接尾辞

□ -able	～できる	avail（利用する）	→ available（利用できる）
□ -less	～がない	flaw（欠点）	→ flawless（欠点がない）
□ -ful	～に満ちた	respect（敬意）	→ respectful（敬意に満ちた）

動詞を作る接尾辞

□ -fy	～にする	simple（簡単な）	→ simplify（簡略化する）
□ -ize	～にする	Western（西洋の）	→ Westernize（西洋化する）
□ -en	～にする	loose（緩い）	→ loosen（緩める）

副詞を作る接尾辞

□ -ward	～の方へ	north（北）	→ northward（北方へ）
□ -ly	～に	deliberate（意図的な）	→ deliberately（意図的に）

TOEIC® TEST
英文法・語彙 模擬試験

最後に、復習とTOEICへの実践準備を兼ねて、総仕上げテストに挑戦しましょう。問題は本番のPart5（40問）、Part6（12問）と同じ数だけあります。実際の試験を想定して、1問20秒、合計17分20秒で解答するようにしてください。なお、「正解と解説」は、202ページ以降にあります。

PRE-TRAINING

Question 1-40 are imcomplete sentences. Four words or phrases, marked (A), (B), (C), (D), are given beneath each sentence. You are to choose the **one** word or phrase that best completes the sentence.

1. Young volunteers often question ------- if raising money and donating it all does more good than traveling across the globe to volunteer.
    (A) itself
    (B) themselves
    (C) they
    (D) their

2. These days more and more employers are ------- older workers for their experience and dedication to the workplace.
    (A) seeks
    (B) sought
    (C) seek
    (D) seeking

3. There are certain tax advantages that are ------- to corporations but simply are not accessible to individuals.
    (A) available
    (B) responsible
    (C) inadequate
    (D) repeated

4. There are concerns about deflation in Japan, where prices have been constantly ------- for months.
    (A) falling
    (B) fall
    (C) fallen
    (D) falls

5. The talents of the hotel's acclaimed chef, restaurateur, architect and designers are expressed through ------- culinary feats.
   (A) theirs
   (B) them
   (C) they
   (D) their

6. The stock market ------- Friday as better-than-expected data gave investors hope of a turnaround in the economy.
   (A) recovering
   (B) recover
   (C) recovery
   (D) recovered

7. The SpaceSaver bike will retail for around $200 ------- it hits the streets on October 18.
   (A) though
   (B) that
   (C) when
   (D) so

8. The productivity growth starting in the mid 1990s helped ------- the natural rate of unemployment.
   (A) lowers
   (B) low
   (C) lower
   (D) lowered

9. The PlayCom Group will continue to ------- on its technology, which has been developed through combining the advanced with long-standing traditions.
   (A) draw
   (B) touch
   (C) play
   (D) put

10. The economic crisis this year -------- to put the venerable company out of business.
    (A) threat
    (B) threatened
    (C) threaten
    (D) threatening

11. The company's first-quarter profit more than ------- year on year because of strong sales from the newly released product.
    (A) doubly
    (B) doubled
    (C) double
    (D) doubling

12. The city of Utsunomiya can be accessed ------- in about 90 minutes by express train from Tokyo, or in about 60 minutes aboard a bullet train.
    (A) easily
    (B) easy
    (C) ease
    (D) easiness

13. The automaker spotted the economic slowdown early in the year and quickly moved to reduce ---- without sacrificing growth opportunities.
  (A) fares
  (B) tolls
  (C) savings
  (D) costs

14. Same-store sales, or sales at stores open at least a year, ------- a key indicator of retailer performance.
  (A) does
  (B) is
  (C) do
  (D) are

15. ------- on our "Customer First" philosophy, we develop and provide high quality products and services that meet a wide variety of customers' demands.
  (A) Based
  (B) Base
  (C) Basing
  (D) Basement

16. Please return your company ID card to your boss, and don't forget to ------- up all your personal belongings.
  (A) show
  (B) get
  (C) pick
  (D) make

17. Nationally, the home value rate of decline stayed nearly flat, ------- about 11 percent according to the research agency.
   (A) at
   (B) to
   (C) in
   (D) on

18. Mr. Foxman has been a valued employee to our office, and we ------- regret the need for his dismissal.
   (A) true
   (B) truth
   (C) truthful
   (D) truly

19. Mortgage rates ------- after the latest news reports suggested the economy may be approaching the bottom of the recession.
   (A) risen
   (B) rising
   (C) rose
   (D) rises

20. Maxpower Corp., one of the area's largest auto parts makers, was ------- in 1935, and today manufactures various auto parts in five states.
   (A) founding
   (B) found
   (C) foundation
   (D) founded

21. Japan Fabric Corp. will ------- its Annual Winter Sale from January 31 to February 11 at the Majesty Hotel in Los Angeles.
   (A) find
   (B) hold
   (C) meet
   (D) see

22. It is generally believed that the more time workers spend without a job, the less ------- they become to potential employers.
   (A) attracted
   (B) attract
   (C) attractive
   (D) attraction

23. In order to ------- the critical issue of environmental preservation, AutoTech Co. continues to develop alternative energy technologies.
   (A) addressing
   (B) addressed
   (C) address
   (D) addresses

24. It is widely expected ------- the central bank will hold interest rates steady at near zero until the end of this year.
   (A) which
   (B) that
   (C) where
   (D) what

25. In a recent study, researchers asked participants how the economic downturn -------- their views on saving for retirement.
    (A) effect
    (B) affect
    (C) affected
    (D) affection

26. If you have any problems using our shopping system, please call us ------- free at 1-800-123-1234, and we will be happy to assist you.
    (A) toll
    (B) price
    (C) fee
    (D) fare

27. If full payment is not received within the next five days, we will have to ------- your account as per company policy.
    (A) suspend
    (B) suspense
    (C) suspension
    (D) supending

28. HeatSaver furnaces emit nearly 15 percent less greenhouse gas ------- oil furnaces.
    (A) as
    (B) than
    (C) to
    (D) that

29. Germany's exports rose nine percent in August over the previous month, ------- they were down from a year earlier.
 (A) otherwise
 (B) because
 (C) though
 (D) which

30. Fast Com Co. believes that a successfull business ------- by individuals who are both pragmatic and creative.
 (A) is leading
 (B) leads
 (C) is led
 (D) led

31. During the first quarter, Super E-Mart lost $58.2 million mainly ------- an increase in provision for loan losses.
 (A) in order to
 (B) due to
 (C) so that
 (D) because

32. Dr. Bright has advocated for a long time that we should take a ------- approach when learning or teaching how to use a foreign language.
 (A) communicated
 (B) communicate
 (C) communication
 (D) communicative

33. Disability is defined as any mental or physical illness or injury ------- prevents you from performing your regular or customary work.
 (A) what
 (B) who
 (C) where
 (D) which

34. Customers must open a new account with SaveFaster Bank and deposit at least $50 ------- eligible for the promotion.
 (A) being
 (B) to be
 (C) to have been
 (D) been

35. Customer demands change constantly. ------- Tomida Tech Co. continues to evolve and provide the innovative services customers want.
 (A) Therefore
 (B) Besides
 (C) Though
 (D) Briefly

36. Consumers are shopping at second-hand stores in growing numbers, -------- luxuries, and putting money in the bank.
 (A) putting on
 (B) cutting in
 (C) cutting back on
 (D) putting up with

37. Auto India Co. said Monday it has failed ------- due payments to policyholders in 897cases totaling about $65 million.
   (A) make
   (B) making
   (C) made
   (D) to make

38. At our Tokyo branch, Japanese-speaking counselors can ------- issues and answer your questions directly.
   (A) discuss
   (B) discuss on
   (C) discussing
   (D) discuss about

39. After considering several candidates, the section manager decided to invite a ------- sales rep for the next seminar for the sales promotion.
   (A) prominent
   (B) prominence
   (C) promotive
   (D) promotion

40. A suitable candidate for the position is a person ------- has experience in sales in the hotel or travel industry.
   (A) whom
   (B) which
   (C) who
   (D) what

Question41-52: Read the texts on the following pages. A word or phrase is missing in some of the sentences. Four answer choices are given below each of these sentences. You are to choose the one word or phrase that best completes the sentence.

Questions 41-43 refer to the following article.

Fire Destroys Value Inn in Tabeto

A fire that broke out on Aug. 6 destroyed a popular inn in the city of Tabeto. No injuries or fatalities were reported. The fire consumed about 5,600 square meters of Value Inn, ------- the main building and a wing in the historical hot spring resort

41. (A) concluding
    (B) concluded
    (C) including
    (D) included

area.

The inn ------- large numbers of tourists over the years with its well known hot

42. (A) attracted
    (B) prevented
    (C) founded
    (D) decreased

spring spa, which had just been renovated last year. The fire started at around 7 A.M. and was put out about 6 hours and 20 minutes -------.

43. (A) latest
    (B) lately
    (C) late
    (D) later

Many tours were cancelled as a result of the conflagration, and many residents in Tabeto are worried about the economic impact the closure of the inn will have.

Questions 44-46 refer to the following letter.

Maeda Foods Co.
4-12-4, Makehami, Chiba City, 275 -9999, Japan

June 11

Owen Freedkin, Operation Manager
FOOD PROCESSING DIVISION
8766 Freedom Blvd,
Los Angeles, CA 902104

Dear Mr. Freedkin:

All of us here at Maeda Foods Co. would like to ------- our hearty congratulations on

44. (A) exclude
(B) extend
(C) expect
(D) export

the establishment of your new venture. We are all impressed by your idea of improving the efficiency of food processing by using the latest scientific developments.

We hope that our two companies can begin ------- business and establish a long-term

45. (A) do
(B) done
(C) did
(D) doing

relationship across the Pacific.

If we can help you in any way, please let me know. We would be very glad to help you try out your ------- idea here in our country.

46. (A) innovative
(B) indecisive
(C) inclusive
(D) interrelated

Sincerely,

Hiroshi Maeda
Food Processing Division
Maeda Foods Co.

Questions 47-49 refer to the following e-mail.

To: Emma Owen<emmaO@paypay.com>
From: Tamako Ishino<TamaIshi@koguma.jp>
Sent: Monday, January 7
Subject: Annual Winter Sale

Dear Ms. Owen,
Thank you for shopping at Koguma. I mailed you to inform you ------- our special

47. (A) at
(B) of
(C) in
(D) through

limited sale for our valued customers.
Koguma Fabrics Co. will hold its Annual Winter Sale from February 1 to 11 at the Rainbow Hotel ballroom in Taipei.
During this campaign we will offer customers a wide selection of our formal party dresses at very ------- prices. Since you are a preferred client, you are also invited

48. (A) competed
(B) competition
(C) compete
(D) competitive

to attend our pre-sale bargain on January 15, with discounts up to 35% on all dresses.
I have attached a catalog file to show you our wide selection. Please check the price list on the pre-sale-bargain page to see the outstanding prices available to customers like you.
Please don't miss this great opportunity, as we perform this type of campaign only once a year. We hope that this will be one ------- that we can repay you for your

49. (A) occasion
(B) potential
(C) charge
(D) stock

patronization over the years.

Yours sincerely,

Tamako Ishino
Managing Director

Questions 50-52 refer to the following e-mail.

From: Cole Bluestone<bluestone@SHSH.com>
To: Bryan Hipple<hipple@SHSH.com>
Subject :September Sales Report
Date: October 10

Total sales in September were less than 1 percent below August sales, but down 9.3 percent from September 2009.
Market demand is ------ weak this year, especially for luxury furniture.

    50. (A) considerate
      (B) considerately
      (C) considerable
      (D) considerably

Also, competition in the marketplace ------- intensifying. LuxMax and ThriftHome

    51. (A) had been
      (B) have been
      (C) will have been
      (D) has been

both launched aggressive sales campaigns last month.
As you know we are in the process of reorganizing our sales department in order to reinforce our sales efforts. Also, we are going to lower the prices of some items as a promotion to attract more customers.
Because of these efforts, we are ------- that sales will return to last year's level by

    52. (A) pessimism
      (B) optimistic
      (C) pessimistic
      (D) optimism

the end of this year.
Attached are the specifications for the reorganization of the sales department.

Cole Bluestone
Sales Manager

正解と解説

1. 正解 (B)

【解説】この文でのquestionは「問いかける」という意味の他動詞として使われている。その目的語が主語と同一であると考えて、再帰代名詞のthemselvesが正解。

構造 Young volunteers(S) (often) question(V) themselves(O) [if [raising money] and [donating it all] does more good (than [traveling (across the globe) (to volunteer)])].

【訳】若いボランティアはお金を工面し、それをすべて寄付することが、ボランティアをするために世界中を回るよりもよいことなのではないかとしばしば自問する。

- ☐ raise money 熟お金を工面する　　☐ donate 動寄付する　　☐ do good 熟ためになる
- ☐ globe 名地球

2. 正解 (D)

【解説】直前にbe動詞があるので、進行形か受動態を予測するが、受動態では文の意味が通じないので、進行形を作る現在分詞形を選ぶ。

構造 (These days) more and more employers(S) are seeking(V) older workers(O) (for their experience and dedication ⟨to the workplace⟩).

【訳】最近より多くの雇用者は経験が豊富で、職場に対する献身度が高いために年配の労働者を求めている。

- ☐ employer 名雇用者　　☐ dedication 名献身　　☐ workplace 名職場

3. 正解 (A)

【解説】「利用できる；手に入る」という意味の形容詞availableを使うと意味が通じる。

構造 There are(V) certain tax advantages(S) ⟨that are available (to corporations)⟩ but (simply) are not accessible (to individuals)⟩.

【訳】個人に対しては全く適応されないが企業には適応される納税のメリットがある。

- ☐ **responsible** 形責任がある　　☐ **inadequate** 形不十分な　　☐ **repeated** 形繰り返しの
- ☐ **accessible** 形利用可能な

4. 正解 (A)

【解説】have been Vingという現在完了進行形の形を使うと意味が通る。この形は「ずっと……している」という継続の意味で使われる。

構造 There are(V) concerns(S) ⟨about deflation⟩ (in Japan, ⟨where prices have been (constantly) falling (for months)⟩).

【訳】日本においてはデフレが懸念されており、物価は数ヶ月間、継続して落ち続けている。

- ☐ concern 名懸念　　☐ deflation 名デフレ　　☐ constantly 副絶えず

5. 正解 (D)

【解説】culinary feat という名詞を修飾する部分に空所があるため、「彼らの」という意味の所有格 their が適当。

構造 [The talents]ⓢ〈of the hotel's acclaimed chef, restaurateur, architect and designers〉 are expressedⓥ (through their culinary feats).

【訳】ホテルのすばらしいシェフ、料理店主、建築家、そしてデザイナーの才能は料理の素晴らしさを通じて表現されている。

- □ talent ⓜ才能
- □ acclaimed ⓜ定評のある
- □ restaurateur ⓜ料理店主
- □ architect ⓜ建築家
- □ culinary ⓜ料理の
- □ feat ⓜ離れ業

6. 正解 (D)

【解説】the stock market を主語とする動詞の部分に空所がある。現在形だと三単現の s が必要なため、この文では過去形を選ぶとよい。

構造 [The stock market]ⓢ recoveredⓥ (Friday)(as better-than-expected data gave investors hope〈of a turnaround 〈in the economy〉〉).

【訳】予測よりも好調なデータが、経済回復の希望を投資家たちに与えたので、株式市場は金曜日に好転した。

- □ recovering recover の現在分詞形
- □ recover ⓜ回復する
- □ recovery ⓜ取り戻すこと
- □ stock market ⓜ株式市場
- □ better-than-expected ⓜ予想を上回る

7. 正解 (C)

【解説】前後の節をつなぐ接続詞を選ぶ問題。前後の文の意味から、「……するとき」という意味で、時を表す when という接続詞を選ぶ。

構造 [The SpaceSaver bike]ⓢ will retailⓥ (for around $200)(when it hits the streets (on October 18)).

【訳】The SpaceSaver 社の自転車はそれが 10 月 18 日に路上に登場したときには約 200 ドルで販売される。

- □ though ⓜ……だけれども
- □ that ⓜ……ということ
- □ so ⓜその結果
- □ so ⓜ……ので
- □ around ⓜおよそ
- □ hit the streets ⓜ発売される

8. 正解 (C)

【解説】help という動詞は直後に原形動詞を置き、help V という形で「V するのに役立つ」という意味で使うことができる。また、help to V という形で、to 不定詞をとることもある。

構造 [The productivity growth]ⓢ〈starting (in the mid 1990s)〉helpedⓥ lower the natural rate〈of unemployment〉.

【訳】1990 年の半ばに始まった生産における成長は自然失業率を低下させる働きをした。

- □ lower ⓜ低下させる
- □ low ⓜ低い
- □ lowered lower の過去(分詞)形
- □ natural rate of unemployment ⓜ自然失業率

9. 正解 (A)

【解説】draw on ~ は「~に頼る」という意味の重要表現。「~に頼る」という意味の表現としては、他に depend on ~、rely on ~ がある。

構造 The PlayCom Group ₍ₛ₎ will continue ₍ᵥ₎ [₍ₒ₎ to draw on its technology, ⟨which has been developed (through [combining the advanced with long-standing traditions])⟩].

【訳】The PlayCom Groupは古くからの伝統と最新技術を組み合わせることを通して開発された技術を最大限に活用し続けるだろう。

□ touch on ~	熟~に触れる	□ play on ~	熟~につけ込む	□ put on	熟着る
□ combine	動組み合わせる	□ long-standing	形長年続いている	□ tradition	名伝統

10. 正解 (B)

【解説】threaten は「~を脅かす」という意味で使われることが多いが、threaten to V というように不定詞を伴うと「Vするおそれがある」という意味になる。

構造 The economic crisis this year ₍ₛ₎ threatened ₍ᵥ₎ to put the venerable company (out of business).

【訳】今年の経済危機は老舗の企業を倒産に追い込みそうになった。

□ threat	名脅し	□ threaten	動脅す	□ threatening	threatenの現在分詞形
□ crisis	名危機	□ venerable	形由緒ある	□ put ~ out of business	熟~を廃業させる

11. 正解 (B)

【解説】double は「倍増する」という意味の動詞としても用いられる。more than double で「倍以上に増加する」という意味になる。

構造 The company's first-quarter profit ₍ₛ₎ more than doubled ₍ᵥ₎ (year on year) (because of strong sales) ⟨from the newly released product⟩.

【訳】その企業の第1四半期の利益は、新しく販売された製品の好調な売り上げのおかげで、前年比で2倍以上になった。

□ doubly	副2倍に	□ double	動2倍になる	□ doubling	doubleの現在分詞形
□ year on year	副前年比で	□ newly	副新たに		

12. 正解 (A)

【解説】文構造に影響しない部分が空所なので、副詞のeasilyを選べばよい。be accessedは受動態。

構造 The city ₍ₛ₎ ⟨of Utsunomiya⟩ can be accessed ₍ᵥ₎ (easily) (in about 90 minutes) (by express train) (from Tokyo), or (in about 60 minutes) (aboard a bullet train).

【訳】宇都宮市は東京から急行電車で約90分で、新幹線で約60分で簡単にアクセスすることができる。

□ easy	形容易な	□ ease	名楽	□ easiness	名容易さ
□ express train	名急行電車	□ aboard	前~に乗って	□ bullet train	名新幹線

13. 正解 (D)

【解説】fareは「運賃」、tollは「通行料金」、savingは「預金」、costは「費用」という意味なので、文意にあったcostsを選ぶ。

構造　The automaker ⓢ spotted ⓥ the economic slowdown ⓞ (early in the year) and (quickly) moved ⓥ (to reduce costs) (without [sacrificing growth opportunities]).

【訳】その自動車メーカーは今年の早い段階で経済の停滞に気づき、すぐに成長機会を犠牲にすることなくコストをカットした。

- □ automaker ㊂自動車メーカー
- □ spot ㊖見つける
- □ slowdown ㊂低迷
- □ sacrifice ㊖犠牲にする
- □ opportunity ㊂機会

14. 正解 (D)

【解説】主語に合った動詞を選ぶ問題。主語のSame-store salesは複数名詞なので、areというbe動詞を選べばよい。「する」という意味では文意が通じないのでdoやdoesは不可。

構造　Same-store sales ⓢ, or ⌈sales⌉ ⟨at ⌈stores⌉ ⟨open at least a year⟩⟩, are ⓥ ⌈a key indicator⌉ ⓒ ⟨of retailer performance⟩.

【訳】既存店、または少なくとも1年間店舗販売をしている店の売り上げは、小売販売実績を把握するための重要な指針だ。

- □ same-store ㊗既存店の
- □ indicator ㊂指針
- □ retailer ㊂小売業者

15. 正解 (A)

【解説】based on ~は「~に基づいて」という意味の表現で、分詞構文として副詞的に用いることができる。baseはもともと「基礎を形成する」という意味の動詞。

構造　(Based on our "Customer First" philosophy), we ⓢ develop and provide ⓥ ⌈high quality products and services⌉ ⓒ ⟨that meet a wide variety of customers' demands⟩.

【訳】「顧客第一主義」の哲学に基づいて、私たちは顧客の幅広い要求を満たす高い品質とサービスを生み出し、提供している。

- □ philosophy ㊂哲学
- □ quality ㊂品質
- □ meet ㊖満たす

16. 正解 (C)

【解説】show upは「現れる」、get upは「起きる」、make upは「化粧をする」という意味なので、文意に合ったpick up（片付ける）を選ぶ。

構造　(Please) return ⓥ your company ID card ⓞ (to your boss), and don't forget ⓥ [ⓞ to pick up all your personal belongings].

【訳】上司に社員証を提出してください。そして持ち物すべてを片づけることを忘れないでください。

- □ ID ㊂身元確認
- □ forget to V ㊘Vするのを忘れる
- □ belongings ㊂所有物

17. 正解 (A)

【解説】割合や時刻などがある点にあることを示す場合にはatという前置詞を使用する。

構造 (Nationally), the home value rate ⟨of decline⟩ stayed (nearly) flat, (at about 11 percent) (according to the research agency).

【訳】調査会社によれば、国全体で家の資産価値の低下はほとんど横ばい状態になっており、約11パーセントということだ。

□ nationally 副全国的に見て　　□ flat 形均一の

18. 正解 (D)

【解説】文構造に影響しない部分に空所があるので、副詞のtruly（心から）を選べばよい。trulyという副詞はregretという動詞を修飾している。

構造 Mr. Foxman has been a valued employee (to our office), and we (truly) regret the need ⟨for his dismissal⟩.

【訳】Foxman氏は私たちの事務所にとって非常に価値のある従業員であり、私たちは彼を解雇しなければならないことを心から残念に思う。

□ true 形真実の　　　　　　□ truth 名真理　　　　　　□ truthful 形誠実な
□ valued 形貴重な　　　　　□ dismissal 名解雇

19. 正解 (C)

【解説】Mortgage ratesを主語とする述語動詞の部分に空所があるので、動詞を選ぶが、主語は複数形なので、三単現のsがついたものは不可。過去形のroseが正解。

構造 Mortgage rates rose (after the latest news reports suggested [the economy may be approaching the bottom ⟨of the recession⟩]).

【訳】最新ニュースによって経済状況の景気後退が底を打ちつつあるという報道がなされた後、住宅ローンの利率が上がった。

□ rise 動上がる　　　　　　□ rising riseの現在分詞形　　□ mortgage 名住宅ローン
□ latest 形最新の　　　　　□ approach 動近づく　　　　　□ recession 名景気後退

20. 正解 (D)

【解説】foundは「設立する」という意味の他動詞。直前にbe動詞があること、また、主語のMaxpower Corpとの関係から、受動態を作る過去分詞形が適切だと考える。

構造 Maxpower Corp., one ⟨of the area's largest auto parts makers⟩, was founded (in 1935), and (today) manufactures various auto parts (in five states).

【訳】地域の最も巨大な自動車の部品メーカーの1つであるMaxpower社は1935年に設立され、現在5つの州で自動車の様々な自動車の部品を製造している。

□ founding foundの現在分詞形　　□ found 動設立する　　□ foundatiion 名設立
□ auto 名自動車　　　　　　　　　□ manufacture 動製造する

21. 正解 (B)

【解説】何かの会を「開催する」と言いたい場合には、holdという動詞を用いる。hold an athletic meeting（体育競技会を開催する）のような表現でも用いられる。

構造 Japan Fabric Corp._(S) will hold_(V) its Annual Winter Sale_(O) (from January 31 to February 11) (at the Majesty Hotel ⟨in Los Angeles⟩).

【訳】Japan Fabric社は年次の冬の販売を1月31日から2月11日までロサンゼルスのMajestyホテルで開催するだろう。

- ☐ find　動見つけ出す　　　　☐ meet　動会う　　　　　　　　☐ see　動見る
- ☐ annual　形年1回の

22. 正解 (C)

【解説】「the+比較級〜, the+比較級.....」は「〜すればするほど.....」の意味。もともとの形は、They become attractive. で、補語の形容詞が前に出て、lessに修飾されていると考えるとよい。

構造 It_(S) is (generally) believed_(V) [that (the more time workers spend without a job), the less attractive they become to potential employers].

【訳】一般的に労働者に仕事がない状況が続けば続くほど、潜在的な雇用者たちにとって彼らは魅力的でなくなる。

- ☐ attracted　attractの過去(分詞)形　　☐ attract　動引きつける　　☐ attraction　名魅力
- ☐ time worker　名時間給労働者　　　　☐ potential　形潜在的な

23. 正解 (C)

【解説】in order to Vは「Vするために」という意味の不定詞の表現。toの直後には原形動詞が置かれる。addressは「取り組む」の意味。

構造 (In order to address the critical issue ⟨of environmental preservation⟩), AutoTech Co._(S) continues_(V) [_(O)to develop alternative energy technologies].

【訳】環境保護という重大な問題に対応するために、AutoTech社は代替エネルギー技術を開発し続けている。

- ☐ addressing　addressの現在分詞形　　☐ addressed　addressの過去(分詞)形　　☐ critical　形重大な
- ☐ environmental　形環境の　　　　　　☐ preservation　名保護
- ☐ alternative energy　名代替エネルギー

24. 正解 (B)

【解説】主語となっているItは形式主語だと考えられる。このitが指す名詞のカタマリとなる部分を作るには、後ろの節をまとめて名詞節を作る接続詞のthatが適切。

構造 It_(S) is (widely) expected_(V) [that the central bank will hold interest rates steady (at near zero) (until the end ⟨of this year⟩)].

【訳】中央銀行は今年の末までゼロ近くで利率を安定させることを広く期待されている。

- ☐ expect　動期待する　　　☐ hold O C　OをCの状態にしておく　　☐ interest rate　名利率
- ☐ steady　形安定した

25. 正解 (C)

【解説】the economic downturn に対応する述語動詞となる動詞を選ぶ。主節の動詞が過去形なので、やはり過去形の affected が正解となる。effect は「影響」、affection は「愛情」という意味の名詞。

構造 (In a recent study), researchers ⓢ asked ⓥ participants ⓞ [ⓞ how the economic downturn affected their views 〈on [saving (for retirement)]〉].

【訳】最近行われた研究において、研究者は参加者に経済の低下が退職のための蓄えに関する考え方にどのような影響を与えたかを質問した。

- □ affect ⓥ 影響する
- □ researcher ⓝ 研究者
- □ saving ⓝ 蓄え；貯蓄

26. 正解 (A)

【解説】toll は「通話料」や「通行料金」を表す名詞。toll free は「無料で」という意味で、副詞句となっている。price は「価格」fee は「謝礼；手数料」fare は「運賃」という意味。

構造 (If you have any problems using our shopping system), please call ⓥ us ⓞ (toll free) (at 1-800-123-1234), and we ⓢ will be ⓥ happy ⓒ to assist you.

【訳】もし私たちのショッピングのシステムを使っていて何らかの問題がありましたら、フリーダイヤル 1-800-123-1234 までお電話ください。喜んでお手伝いさせていただきます。

27. 正解 (A)

【解説】have to V は「V しなければならない」という意味で、V の部分には常に原形動詞が置かれるので suspend（一時停止する）が正解。suspense は「不安」、suspension は「中止」という意味の名詞。

構造 (If full payment is not received (within the next five days)), we ⓢ will have to suspend ⓥ your account ⓞ (as per company policy).

【訳】もしこの 5 日以内で全額の支払いがなければ、私たちは企業の方針としてあなたの口座を停止しなくてはならない。

- □ suspense ⓝ 不安
- □ suspension ⓝ 中止
- □ suspending suspend の現在分詞形
- □ payment ⓝ 支払い
- □ as per 〜 ⓘ 〜に従って
- □ policy ⓝ 方針

28. 正解 (B)

【解説】less は little の比較級で「より少ない」という意味。比較級の直後に続けて、「〜よりも」という意味で、比較対象を表す場合には than を用いる。

構造 HeatSaver furnaces ⓢ emit ⓥ nearly 15 percent less greenhouse gas ⓞ (than oil furnaces).

【訳】HeatSaver 炉は石油を燃料にする釜よりもほぼ 15 パーセント温室効果ガスの排出を抑える。

- □ furnace ⓝ 暖房炉
- □ emit ⓥ 放つ
- □ greenhouse gas ⓝ 温室効果ガス

29. 正解 (C)
【解説】8月に輸出額が上昇したという主節の内容と、前年度より減少したという従属節の内容は逆の方向性なので、逆接の意味の接続詞though（.....だけれども）が正解となる。

構造 Germany's exports ⓢ rose ⓥ (nine percent) (in August) (over the previous month), (though they were down (from a year earlier)).

【訳】ドイツの輸出高は、前年同期よりも低いとはいえ、先月に比べ、8月に9パーセント上昇した。

☐ otherwise 副さもなければ　　☐ because 接.....だから　　☐ export 名輸出高

30. 正解 (C)
【解説】空所に入る動詞の主語となるa successful businessは「導かれた」と考えるのが適当なので、受動態のis ledが正解となる。

構造 Fast Com Co. ⓢ believes ⓥ [ⓞ that a successfull business is led (by individuals ⟨who are both pragmatic and creative⟩)].

【訳】Fast Com社のビジネスの成功は、実践的かつ創造性のある個人によって導かれるものであると信じている。

☐ leads 動導く　　☐ led leadの過去（分詞）形　　☐ both A and B 熟AとBの両方
☐ pragmatic 形実践的な　　☐ creative 形創造力のある

31. 正解 (B)
【解説】直後に名詞をおき、理由を表す場合には、前置詞句のdue to ～（～のために）やbecause of ～が用いられる。

構造 (During the first quarter), Super E-Mart ⓢ lost ⓥ $58.2 million ⓞ (mainly) (due to an increase ⟨in provision ⟨for loan losses⟩⟩).

【訳】第1四半期の間、Super E-Martは主に貸付損失の引当金の増加のため、5820万ドルを失った。

☐ in order to V 熟Vするために　　☐ so that 接.....するために　　☐ because 接なぜなら
☐ mainly 副主に　　☐ provision for loan loss 名貸倒引当金

32. 正解 (D)
【解説】approachという名詞を修飾する部分に空所があるため、形容詞のcommunicative（伝達の）を選ぶ。

構造 Dr. Bright ⓢ has advocated ⓥ (for a long time) [ⓞ that we should take a communicative approach (when learning or teaching [how to use a foreign language])].

【訳】Bright博士は外国語の使い方について学習したり教えたりするときに、コミュニケーション重視の手法をとるべきだと長い間主張している。

☐ communicated communicateの過去（分詞）形　　☐ communicate 動伝達する
☐ communication 名伝達　　☐ advocate 動主張する　　☐ approach 名方法

33. 正解 (D)

【解説】先行詞となる名詞は物を表す言葉で、直後には動詞が続いているため、関係代名詞の主格のwhichを選べばよい。

構造 Disability₍ₛ₎ is defined₍ᵥ₎ (as any mental or physical illness or injury) ⟨which prevents you (from performing your regular or customary work)⟩.

【訳】障害とは、規則的、習慣的な仕事を遂行することを妨げるような心理的、肉体的な病気やけがとして定義されている。

- □ disability 名障害
- □ physical 形肉体の
- □ customary 形習慣的な
- □ define A as B 熟AをBと定義する
- □ illness 名病気
- □ mental 形精神の
- □ injury 名負傷

34. 正解 (B)

【解説】不定詞は、「Vするために」という意味で、「目的」を表すことができる。be動詞の場合には、原形のbeを用いto beという形になる。

構造 Customers₍ₛ₎ must open₍ᵥ₎ a new account₍ₒ₎ ⟨with SaveFaster Bank⟩ and deposit₍ᵥ₎ at least $50₍ₒ₎ (to be eligible (for the promotion)).

【訳】キャンペーンの対象となるためには、顧客はSaveFaster銀行に新しい口座を開いて少なくとも50ドルを預けなければならない。

- □ deposit 動預金する
- □ promotion 名助成

35. 正解 (A)

【解説】顧客の要求の変化は、Tomida Tech社が進化し続ける「理由」なので、順接の意味で文をつなぎ「それ故に」という意味になるthereforeという接続副詞を選ぶ。

構造 Customer demands₍ₛ₎ change₍ᵥ₎ (constantly). (Therefore) Tomida Tech Co.₍ₛ₎ continues₍ᵥ₎ [₀ to evolve and provide the innovative services ⟨customers want⟩].

【訳】顧客の要求は常に変化している。それ故にTomida Tech社は進化し、顧客が求める革新的なサービスを提供し続けている。

- □ besides 副その上
- □ evolve 動進化する
- □ though 接……だけれども
- □ innovative 形革新的な
- □ briefly 副簡潔に

36. 正解 (C)

【解説】cut back on ~は「~を切りつめる」という意味。cut inは「割り込む」、put onは「身につける」、put up with ~は「~を我慢する」という意味。

構造 Consumers₍ₛ₎ are shopping₍ᵥ₎ (at second-hand stores) (in growing numbers), (cutting back on luxuries, and putting money (in the bank)).

【訳】消費者はますます中古品店で買い物をしており、贅沢を切り詰め、銀行に貯金をしている。

- □ second-hand 形中古品を扱う
- □ luxury 名贅沢品

37. 正解 (D)

【解説】failという動詞の直後には不定詞が続き、fail to Vで「Vできない」という意味になる。

構造 Auto India Co.ⓢ saidⓥ (Monday) [ⓞ it has failed to make due payments (to policyholders) (in 897cases ⟨totaling about $65 million⟩)].

【訳】Auto India社は総額6500万ドルに及ぶ897件において、保険契約者に対して未払い金を支払うことができなかったと月曜日に公表した。

- ☐ fail to V ㊥ Vできない
- ☐ due ㊗当然支払われるべき
- ☐ policyholder ㊔保険契約者

38. 正解 (A)

【解説】canという助動詞の後ろには原形動詞が置かれる。discuss（話し合う）という動詞は他動詞なので、直後に名詞となる目的語が続き前置詞は必要ない。

構造 (At our Tokyo branch), Japanese-speaking counselorsⓢ can discussⓥ issuesⓞ and answerⓥ your questionsⓞ (directly).

【訳】我々の東京支店では、日本語の話せるカウンセラーが問題点について話し合い、あなたの質問に直接お答えします。

- ☐ Japanese-speaking ㊗日本語を話す
- ☐ counselor ㊔カウンセラー

39. 正解 (A)

【解説】sales repという名詞を修飾する部分が空所なので、形容詞のprominent（卓越した）が正解。

構造 (After considering several candidates), the section managerⓢ decidedⓥ [ⓞ to invite a prominent sales rep (for the next seminar ⟨for the sales promotion⟩)].

【訳】何名かの候補者を考慮した後、部署のリーダーは営業のための次のセミナーに有能な販売員を招待することを決めた。

- ☐ prominence ㊔顕著
- ☐ promotive ㊗促進する
- ☐ promotion ㊔昇進
- ☐ candidate ㊔志願者
- ☐ rep ㊔セールスマン
- ☐ sales promotion ㊔販売促進活動

40. 正解 (C)

【解説】先行詞はa personという人をあらわす名詞。また、空所の直後には動詞が続いていることから、関係代名詞の主格、whoが正解となる。

構造 A suitable candidateⓢ ⟨for the position⟩ isⓥ a personⓒ ⟨who has experience ⟨in sales ⟨in the hotel or travel industry⟩⟩⟩.

【訳】その職にふさわしい志願者はホテルや旅行業界で販売の経験がある人だ。

41. 正解　**(C)**
【解説】include は「含む」という意味の動詞。including 〜は「〜を含めて」という意味で、前置詞のような働きをする。conclude は「終える」という意味なので文の意味に合わない。

42. 正解　**(A)**
【解説】主語の the inn と目的語の tourists を結ぶのに最も適切な意味の動詞は attract（引きつける；魅了する）。prevent は「妨げる」、found は「設立する」、decrease は「減らす」という意味なので、いずれも文の意味に合わない。

43. 正解　**(D)**
【解説】「〜経って」という意味を表すには、〜 later という表現を用いる。latest は形容詞で「最新の」、lately は副詞で「最近」という意味。late は形容詞や副詞として用いられ、「遅い；遅く」という意味。

文構造

Fire Destroys Value Inn ⟨**in Tabeto**⟩

A fire ⟨that broke out (on Aug. 6)⟩ destroyed a popular inn ⟨in the city ⟨of Tabeto⟩. No injuries or fatalities were reported. The fire consumed about 5,600 square meters ⟨of Value Inn⟩, ⟨including the main building and a wing ⟨in the historical hot spring resort area⟩⟩.

The inn attracted large numbers of tourists (over the years) (with its well known hot spring spa, ⟨which had just been renovated (last year)⟩⟩. The fire started (at around 7 A.M.) and was put out (about 6 hours and 20 minutes later).

Many tours were cancelled (as a result ⟨of the conflagration⟩), and many residents ⟨in Tabeto⟩ are worried (about the economic impact ⟨the closure ⟨of the inn⟩ will have⟩⟩.

---- 文章の訳 ----

設問 41 ～ 43 は、次の記事に関するものです。

Tabeto の火災で Value Inn 焼損

　8月6日発生の火災で、Tabeto 市の人気旅館が焼損した。死傷者の報告はない。この火災で、歴史的温泉保養地の本館および翼棟を含む、Value Inn の 5,600 平米が焼失した。
　この旅館は、温泉浴場で知られ、長年にわたり、多くの観光客をひきつけてきた。温泉は、昨年、改修したばかりであった。火災は午前7時ごろ発生し、約6時間 20 分後に鎮火した。
　この大火災のため、多くのツアーが中止となり、Tabeto 市の多くの住民が、この旅館閉鎖の経済的影響について心配している。

◆ ボキャブラリー ◆

☐ fire	名 火災	☐ found	動 設立する
☐ break out	熟 発生する	☐ decrease	動 減らす
☐ injury	名 負傷	☐ renovate	動 改修する
☐ fatality	名 死亡者	☐ put out	熟 鎮火する
☐ consume	動 破壊する	☐ latest	形 最新の
☐ conclude	動 終える	☐ lately	副 最近
☐ including	前 ～を含む	☐ late	形 遅い
☐ include	動 含む	☐ later	副 後で
☐ historical	形 歴史的な	☐ as a result of ～	熟 ～の結果として
☐ hot spring resort	名 温泉保養地	☐ conflagration	名 大火災
☐ attract	動 ひきつける	☐ closure	名 閉鎖
☐ prevent	動 妨げる		

44. 正解 (B)
【解説】ex- という接頭辞で始まる動詞の中から、意味的に文と合っているものを選ぶ。congratulations（祝辞）という目的語の名詞と最もよく結びつくのは extend（延ばす；述べる）。extend congratulations で「祝辞を述べる」という意味になる。exclude は「除外する」、expect は「期待する」、export は「輸出する」という意味。ex- という接頭辞は主に「外」を意味する。

45. 正解 (D)
【解説】begin という他動詞の目的語には、動名詞も不定詞も用いることができる。ここでは動名詞の doing を選べばよい。

46. 正解 (A)
【解説】idea という名詞を修飾し、文意に最も合っている形容詞は innovative（革新的な）。indecisive は「優柔不断な」、inclusive は「包括的な」、interrelated は「相互に関連した」という意味で、いずれも文意に合わない。

文構造

Maeda Foods Co.
4-12-4, Makehami, Chiba City, 275-9999, Japan

June 11

Owen Freedkin, Operation Manager
FOOD PROCESSING DIVISION
8766 Freedom Blvd,
Los Angeles, CA 902104

Dear Mr. Freedkin:

All ⟨of us⟩ ⟨here at Maeda Foods Co.⟩ would like to extend our hearty congratulations ⟨on the establishment ⟨of your new venture⟩⟩. We are all impressed (by your idea ⟨of improving the efficiency ⟨of food processing (by using the latest scientific developments)⟩⟩).

We hope [that our two companies can begin [doing business and establish a long-term relationship ⟨across the Pacific⟩]].

(If we can help you (in any way)), (please) let me know. We would be very glad to help you try out your innovative idea (here) (in our country).

Sincerely,

Hiroshi Maeda
Food Processing Division
Maeda Foods Co.

文章の訳

設問 44 ～ 46 は、次のレターに関するものです。

Maeda Foods Co.
4-12-4, Makehami, Chiba City, 275 -9999, Japan

6月11日

Owen Freedkin, Operation Manager
FOOD PROCESSING DIVISION
8766 Freedom Blvd,
Los Angeles, CA 902104

Freedkin 様

Maeda Foods 社の社員一同、御社の新規ベンチャー事業の発足に対し、心よりのお祝いを申し上げます。最新の科学的発展を活用し、食品加工の効率を改善するという御社の発想に、弊社社員一同、感銘を受けました。

弊社では、我々の二つの会社が事業を開始し、太平洋を横断した長期的関係を築くことができればと希望しております。

私どもにお力添えできることがございましたら、なんなりとご連絡ください。日本で御社の革新的発想を試験運用するためのお手伝いをさせていただければ、誠に幸甚と存じます。

敬具

Hiroshi Maeda
食品加工部
Maeda Foods 社

◆ ボキャブラリー ◆

□ extend congratulations	熟 祝辞を述べる	□ long-term relationship	名 長期的関係
□ exclude	動 除外する	□ the Pacific	名 太平洋
□ expect	動 期待する	□ try out	熟 試験運用する
□ export	動 輸出する	□ innovative	形 革新的な
□ establishment	名 発足	□ indecisive	形 優柔不断な
□ impress	動 感銘を与える	□ inclusive	形 包括的な
□ efficiency	名 効率	□ interrelated	形 相互に関連した
□ food processing	名 食品加工	□ sincerely	副 敬具

47. 正解　**(B)**
【解説】inform A of B は、「AにBを知らせる」という意味の重要表現。Aの部分には、情報を知らせる相手が置かれ、Bの部分には情報が置かれる。

48. 正解　**(D)**
【解説】price（値段）という名詞を修飾し、最も意味が適しているのは、competitive（競争力のある）。compete は動詞で「競争する」という意味。また、competition は名詞で「競争」という意味。

49. 正解　**(A)**
【解説】直後に同格の that 節を伴う名詞で意味が合っているものを選択する。「機会」という意味の occasion が最も適切。potential は「潜在能力」、charge は「料金」、stock は「在庫」という意味なので、いずれも文意に合わない。

To: Emma Owen<emmaO@paypay.com>
From: Tamako Ishino<TamaIshi@koguma.jp>
Sent: Monday, January 7
Subject: Annual Winter Sale

Dear Ms. Owen,

Thank you (for shopping (at Koguma)). I mailed you (to inform you (of our special limited sale) ⟨for our valued customers⟩)).

Koguma Fabrics Co. will hold its Annual Winter Sale (from February 1 to 11) (at the Rainbow Hotel ballroom ⟨in Taipei⟩).

(During this campaign) we will offer customers a wide selection of our formal party dresses (at very competitive prices). (Since you are a preferred client), you are (also) invited to attend our pre-sale bargain ⟨on January 15⟩, ⟨with discounts ⟨up to 35%⟩ ⟨on all dresses⟩⟩.

I have attached a catalog file (to show you our wide selection). (Please) check the price list ⟨on the pre-sale-bargain page⟩ (to see the outstanding prices ⟨available to customers ⟨like you⟩⟩).

(Please) don't miss this great opportunity, (as we perform this type of campaign (only once a year)). We hope [that this will be one occasion ⟨that we can repay you (for your patronization ⟨over the years⟩)⟩].

Yours sincerely,

Tamako Ishino
Managing Director

文章の訳

設問 47 〜 49 は、次のメールに関するものです。

宛先：Emma Owen<emmaO@paypay.com>
差出人：Tamako Ishino<TamaIshi@koguma.jp>
日付：1月7日（月）
件名：年に一度の冬の大売出し

Owen 様

Koguma でお買い上げいただきありがとうございます。当店のお得意様に特別限定売り出しのご案内です。

Koguma Fabrics 社では、2月1日から11日まで、台北、Rainbow Hotel の舞踏会場にて、年に一度の冬の大売出しを開催いたします。

キャンペーン期間中、当店では、豊富な品揃えのパーティー用正装ドレスを、大変お買い得なお値段で、お客様にご提供いたします。また、お客様は優遇顧客として、1月15日に、全ドレスが最大35％引きとなる売り出し前バーゲンへのご参加にも、ご招待いたします。

当店の豊富な品揃えをご覧いただくため、カタログのファイルを添付いたします。売り出し前バーゲンのページの価格表をご確認いただき、お得意様のためのとびきり価格をご覧ください。

当店でのこうしたキャンペーンは年に一度限りですので、この絶好の機会をお見逃しなきようお願い申し上げます。当店では、この売り出しが、お客様からの長年のご愛顧にお応えすることのできる機会のひとつとなればと願っております。

敬具
Tamako Ishino
常務取締役

◆ ボキャブラリー ◆

☐ inform A of B	熟 A に B を知らせる	☐ occasion	名 機会
☐ valued customer	名 お得意様	☐ potential	名 潜在能力
☐ competition	名 競争	☐ charge	名 料金
☐ compete	動 競争する	☐ stock	名 在庫
☐ competitive	形 競争力のある	☐ repay	動 報いる
☐ preferred	形 優遇の	☐ patronization	名 ご愛顧
☐ price list	名 価格表	☐ over the years	熟 長年の
☐ outstanding	形 傑出した	☐ Managing Director	名 常務取締役
☐ miss	動 見逃す		

50. 正解　**(D)**
【解説】よく似た形容詞、副詞の識別の問題。直後の weak という形容詞を修飾している部分なので、副詞が入るとわかる。considerably（かなり）が最も文意に合っている。considerately は「思いやり深く」という意味。

51. 正解　**(D)**
【解説】文の主語は competition という単数名詞なので、have been は適切ではない。また、前後の文は主に現在形で、現状を報告する内容となっていることから、現在完了形の has been が正解となる。

52. 正解　**(B)**
【解説】are という be 動詞の補語となる、optimistic（楽観的な）という形容詞が最も文の内容に適している。that 以下では希望的観測が述べられているため、pessimistic（悲観的な）は文意に合わない。-ism は「..... 主義」という名詞を作る接尾辞で、optimism は「楽観主義」、pessimism は「悲観主義」という意味。

文構造

From: Cole Bluestone<bluestone@SHSH.com>
To: Bryan Hipple<hipple@SHSH.com>
Subject :September Sales Report
Date: October 10

Total sales ⒮ ⟨in September⟩ were ⓥ (less than 1 percent below August sales), but (down 9.3 percent) (from September 2009).

Market demand ⒮ is ⓥ (considerably) weak ⓒ (this year), (especially for luxury furniture).
(Also), competition ⒮ ⟨in the marketplace⟩ has been intensifying ⓥ. LuxMax and ThriftHome ⒮ both launched ⓥ aggressive sales campaigns ⓞ (last month).

(As you know) we ⒮ are ⓥ (in the process ⟨of reorganizing our sales department (in order to reinforce our sales efforts)⟩). (Also), we ⒮ are going to lower ⓥ the prices ⓞ ⟨of some items⟩ (as a promotion ⟨to attract more customers⟩).

(Because of these efforts), we ⒮ are ⓥ optimistic ⓒ [that sales will return (to last year's level) (by the end of this year)].

Attached ⓒ are ⓥ the specifications ⒮ ⟨for the reorganization ⟨of the sales department⟩⟩.

Cole Bluestone
Sales Manager

---- 文章の訳 ----

設問 50 ～ 52 は、次のメールに関するものです。

差出人：Cole Bluestone<bluestone@SHSH.com>
宛先：Bryan Hipple<hipple@SHSH.com>
件名：9月販売報告書
日付：10月10日

9月の全売上は、8月の売上よりも1パーセント少なく、2009年9月からは9.3パーセント下落しました。
今年、とりわけ高級家具において、市場需要はかなりの弱さです。また市場競争も激しさを増しています。LuxMax社およびThriftHome社の両者は、先月、積極的な販売キャンペーンを始めました。
ご存知の通り、販売力を強化するため、当社は営業部の組織改変の途上にあります。また当社は、より多くの顧客をひきつけるための販売促進策として、いくつかの商品の価格を引き下げようとしています。
こうした取り組みにより、販売は今年末までに昨年並みの水準を回復するものと楽観しています。
営業部の組織改変の仕様書を添付いたします。

Cole Bluestone
販売課長

◆ ボキャブラリー ◆

total sales	名全売上	reorganize	動再編成する
below	前〜より少ない	reinforce	動強化する
market demand	名市場需要	attract	動ひきつける
considerately	副思いやり深く	optimism	名楽観主義
considerably	副かなり	optimistic	形楽観的な
competition	名競争	pessimism	名悲観主義
marketplace	名市場	pessimistic	形悲観的な
aggressive	形積極的な	attached	形添付された
as you know	熟ご存知のとおり	specification	名仕様書
in the process of 〜	熟〜の過程で	reorganization	名再編成

●著者紹介

安河内 哲也 Tetsuya Yasukochi

　1967年生まれ。東進ビジネススクール・東進ハイスクール講師、言語文化舎代表。帰国子女でも留学経験者でもないが、TOEIC TESTにおいて、リスニング、リーディング、スピーキング、ライティングすべての分野での満点取得をはじめ、国連英検特A級、英検1級、通訳案内士など多くの英語資格を取得。独自のメソッドを詰め込んだ熱い講義は多くの人から絶賛される。著書は『新TOEIC TEST英文法スピードマスター』『ゼロからスタート　英文法』『ゼロからスタート　リスニング』『小学英語スーパードリル①②③』(以上、Jリサーチ出版)ほか70冊以上に及ぶ。
URLは www.yasukochi.jp

編集協力	佐藤誠司、石塚浩之
カバーデザイン	滝デザイン事務所
本文デザイン&DTP	新藤 昇
英文校正	Miguel Corti

新 TOEIC® TEST 英文法・語彙スピードマスター

平成22年（2010年）　4月10日　　初版第1刷発行
平成22年（2010年）10月10日　　　　第2刷発行

著　者	安河内哲也
発行人	福田富与
発行所	有限会社　Jリサーチ出版
	〒166-0002　東京都杉並区高円寺北2-29-14-705
	電話 03(6808)8801㈹　FAX 03(5364)5310
	編集部 03(6808)8806
	http://www.jresearch.co.jp
印刷所	株式会社シナノパブリッシングプレス

ISBN978-4-86392-008-8　禁無断転載。なお、乱丁・落丁はお取り替えいたします。